ARCO

HOW TO
WRITE

Poetry

D0964301

Nancy Bogen

Associate Professor of English
College of Staten Island
CUNY

MACMILLAN • USA

To my stepson, Edward Greissle

Third Edition

Copyright © 1998, 1994, 1991 by Nancy Bogen
All rights reserved
including the right of reproduction
in whole or in part in any form

Macmillan Reference USA
A Simon & Schuster Macmillan Company
1633 Broadway
New York, NY 10019-6785

An Arco Book

ARCO is a registered trademark of Simon & Schuster, Inc.
MACMILLAN is a registered trademark of Macmillan, Inc.

Manufactured in the United States of America

10 9 8 7 6 5 4 3 2 1

A catalogue record is available from the Library of Congress.

ISBN 0-02-862207-3

CONTENTS

ACKNOWLEDGMENTS

*Grateful thanks are given to the following authors
and publishers:*

"Life's Intricate Blessings"
Copyright © by Lisa Baroz.

"I Heard a Fly Buzz"
Reprinted by permission of the publishers and the Trustees of Amherst College from THE POEMS OF EMILY DICKINSON, Thomas H. Johnson, ed., Cambridge, Mass.: The Belknap Press of Harvard University Press, Copyright 1951, © 1955, 1979, 1983 by the President and Fellows of Harvard College.

"The Development of a Poem"
Copyright © Ruth Fainlight.

"Howl"
Excerpt from HOWL by Allen Ginsberg, edited by Barry Miles. Copyright © 1986, 1956 by Allen Ginsberg. Reprinted by permission of Harper & Row, Publishers, Inc.

"Apothegms and Counsels"
Copyright © Colette Inez, 1977, ALIVE AND TAKING NAMES. Ohio University Press, Athens, OH.

"Skokie River Cadenzas"
Copyright © Colette Inez, 1983, EIGHT MINUTES FROM THE SUN. Saturday Press, Montclair, N.J.

"Shaking His Loose Skin"
Issa, Copyright © tr. by Peter Beilenson and Harry Behn.

"Coconut Grove"
Copyright © Karen Laszlo.

The Iliad
Homer, Copyright © tr. by Richmond Lattimore.

"A Psychic Psyche's Vow to Cupid"
"Wake Up and Smell the Coffee"
Copyright © Joedy Lo Presto.

INTRODUCTION
by Harvey Shapiro

The moment when I decided to write poetry is very clear to me. I was sitting in an outhouse behind the tent I lived in beside an airfield in Foggia, Italy. The year was 1945. My outfit was the 347th Squadron of the 99th Bomb Group of the 15th Air Force. We flew B-17's over targets in Austria and Germany. I was a gunner in that squadron.

It was a spring day of my twentieth year. Sitting in the outhouse, brooding on mortality, reading a paperback copy of Walt Whitman's poems distributed by the armed forces, I was suddenly struck in wonder by whatever it was that allowed patterns of words set down almost a hundred years ago to survive. Survival was on my mind. It was on my third mission, over Vienna or "flak alley" as we used to call it, some months before that I had first realized—I won't go into the details, they don't really matter—I could die, this could be it. Looking at blue sky one minute and the next not. Nothing. A simple truth had been driven home to me: A human being seemed durable but in fact was not. What was it, I thought, that permitted words, mere breath, just air (nonsense syllables really if you repeated them enough times to yourself) to outweather time, to stay intact? More than that, words, scrambled bits of alphabet, when placed in a poem, held a voice inside them that you could clearly hear. Not speaking down the long tunnel of time but at your ear, now, in your living room.

In my case, just then, it was in an outhouse and it was Walt Whitman speaking to me. He always knew he would speak to readers a hundred years hence. Nevertheless, I realized then that I had heard earlier voices—those of Wyatt, Shakespeare, Milton, Donne—in my reading for school and for pleasure. What permitted those words to come through, those voices to resonate in the present air? Art was magical. It must be. Through art, through craft, you could draw a circle around words that would safeguard them from the ravages of time. As the Roman poet Horace boasted (in Ezra Pound's translation): "This monument will outlast metal and I made it."

Brooding on my own mortality, I wanted a shot at that kind of immortality, so I decided to write poetry. And when I returned to college after the war, I switched from an International Relations major (whatever that is or whatever it meant to me) to an English major.

Above all, I wanted to put my experiences during the war into a safeguarding form, to see if I could translate what had happened to me and what I had witnessed into lines that would stay on the page. I had no thought then of a career—what was the career of a poet anyway? Nor did I think about a book with my name on the jacket. I simply wanted to take what I knew and put it into a form that would give it a chance of survival.

I knew I had to study the poetry of the past before trying to write my own, to understand how those voices managed to stay alive, to keep transmitting, across centuries. When I found a poem that performed that magic for me, I would first commit it to memory if I could, then take it apart to see how it was made. If you love something—a car, a painting, a piece of music—your love and admiration increase with your knowledge of how it works and how it was put together.

It took me ten years or so before I could fix into poetry that "death-instructed kid"—myself in the war at twenty. The poem I did it in is called "Battle Report." It's a poem in five sections, the first of which is in blank verse, five iambic feet to the line. I learned that measure from reading Shakespeare, Milton and Wordsworth, counting the syllables and accents. Later my poems came to me mainly in lines of four beats. That seemed more natural for me, and I speculated that perhaps the American line was shorter, moved more quickly than the classic English pentameter, as if it were mirroring our faster speech. Later still, as my subject matter changed and became more anecdotal, and my sense of the line became stronger, I began to work mainly in free verse.

Despite that, in my reading of contemporary poets I was aware of how the exact form and the very sound of a poem written centuries ago can sometimes move a poet of today into something that is not imitation—there is nothing antique about it—but something I would call an equivalence. An outstanding example of this is Robert Lowell's sonorous poem "The Quaker Graveyard in Nantucket." It is written in lines of five beats (accents) mixed with lines of three, and irregularly rhymed. In its form and in its large, open vowel, organ-stop sound it follows Milton's great elegy "Lycidas." And for good reason: Both poems, though centuries apart, are about a comrade drowned at sea.

The American poet George Oppen once told me, when I praised a poem he had written about a woman in a subway car, a very city poem, that it was Sir Thomas Wyatt's sound he was after in those lines. In his case, he was not following any of the forms the 16th century English poet had worked in. But in his own free verse, he was after the same tonal qualities that make Wyatt's lines sing, and he was also after the delicate lyricism and clarity with which Wyatt had depicted women.

Nothing is as mysterious in the writing of poetry as coming upon the opening line. How do you know this is the beginning of a poem? A student in a workshop class of mine at Columbia once asked this of George Oppen, who was my guest there. Oppen said, "You know you have a first line when you can jump up and down on it." In other words, when it can bear some weight, carry a structure, support the fictive world you plan to build.

To shift the metaphor, imagine yourself surfcasting into the Atlantic on a lonely beach in October. There's nothing to see in the ocean, an immense darkness, a nothingness. But teeming you know. You cast again and again and finally there's a strike (and it's always a lucky strike). A surging, living weight is on the end of your line. You can't make out what it is, what it looks like, because it's below the surface. But its energy and power flow back to you along the length of the line. That's like the beginning of a poem. Unmistakable. The words in your head have hooked into something deep in your unconscious. To bring that emotional freight to the light, to master it and understand it, to let it find its own lovely shape in the light, is the making of a poem.

CHAPTER ONE
Getting started

Did you ever get the feeling that you had something to say that was all ready and waiting inside of you? Did you ever then take up a pen or pencil only to find that your writing implement remained immobile, the page in front of you blank—the something inside all bottled up, stuck? It's not very pleasant, is it? It can get you into a real sweat. But even if such a fate never befell you, a little unlocking of your word hoard would not be amiss.

WORDS WORDS WORDS

Few people would quarrel with the idea that the hardest thing about doing anything is getting started. The trouble is that wise, old saying, "Just begin at the beginning," seldom holds true for writing. Beginnings or introductions, one learns with time and experience, are often best left until after a work is in progress.

There is, however, another way of following that rule to good effect, and that is by concentrating on words, the building blocks of writing. "Words, words, words," Hamlet said when the old fool Polonius asked him, "What do you read, my lord?" While the Prince was showing contempt for the courtier's world and its empty palaver, he was no mean user of words himself, as anyone who knows the play will agree.

Later in this book we will look at a perfect example of this in connection with the writing of blank verse, Hamlet's famous soliloquy, "To Be or Not to Be." Right now let's kick off—with words. Your words!

Did you ever wonder what is supposed to be accomplished by the few bounces a basketball player makes before attempting a foul shot or the practice swings a baseball player takes with his bat before a pitch? Certainly not very much in terms of racking up points; the basketball when released may hit the hoop's rim and come careening back, the batter may strike out. But in terms of total performance those dry-run dribbles or swipes in the air accomplish a good deal—they help players get in the "groove." How so? By making them relax, which in turn causes them to focus their whole attention on the matter at hand.

What we are about to do works on the same principle with respect to using words.

EXERCISE 1

If you are using this book in a class and your instructor has encouraged you to acquire a notebook, or if you are going it alone and wish to work in one, turn to the first blank page. Consider "pen," not the pen in your hand, but the word for it. For two minutes let your mind wander where it cares to with "pen," and follow it with your own pen. Jot down as many single words and short phrases as occur to you. If you like to work in columns, by all means do so. But if this turns out to be a problem, do it any old way. Bear in mind that this is not simply an assignment—the person who will be most interested in your list and who stands to benefit most from it is YOU.

When the time is up, add up what you have. Words count one, phrases two. Was your score higher or lower than those of most of the people in your class, or was it around the same? If you're using this book all by your lonesome, you don't have anyone to compare yourself with, so you're all right, right? Right.

What do the different scores prove? Nothing. But how do you FEEL? Like going on? Good.

EXERCISE 2

Turn to a fresh page and for two more minutes do the same thing—with, oh say, "lipstick."

Did you come up with more words and phrases this time or fewer? Generally it's more, considerably more, but if you didn't, not to worry. Just carry on.

EXERCISE 3

Turn the page and try this procedure yet once more, but this time with a word of your own. It can be one for something concrete such as we've already used or for some abstraction like "love."

Did you have even more words and phrases? One tends to have more the second time round, though the rate of increase is generally not as high as before.

If you didn't end up with more or had fewer, could it be that you're not interested in words? What! Not interested in words and you want to write poetry? Impossible! You're just a late bloomer, that's all. Persevere, try old Exercise 3 again a few more times with other words of your own. And then, ONWARD!

Look back over your pages and see if you repeated yourself anywhere; this goes for ideas as well as words. What? You don't like to repeat yourself? Why not? Some of the best writers ever were repeaters in one fashion or another. Look at Shakespeare's Macbeth, for instance:

Tomorrow, and tomorrow, and tomorrow,
Creeps in this petty pace from day to day.

So like it, like it. By the end of this book you'll be repeating yourself all over the place—beautifully!

If you did happen to use the same words or phrases more than once it's all to the good even though you didn't intend to. It shows that there is something on your mind. Now how about that. Maybe you ought to try writing about IT some time . . . but really writing about it. There may be a poem in it. . . .

If you didn't repeat anything, no cause for concern. If not now, you'll have something on your mind before long.

CRAZY WORDS AND WAYS TO USE THEM

If you want to write, especially write poetry, you have to have a feeling for words besides the ability to unlock your hoard of them, just as a budding painter has to have a feeling for color, line, and form. One of the best ways to cultivate this feeling if you don't have it or it's lying dormant somewhere within you is to go a little crazy with words—yes, to get moonstruck with, as, for example, Lewis Carroll did in "Jabberwocky," which turns up amidst Alice's adventures in Through the Looking-Glass. This poem is surely one of the all-time loonies in our language:

'Twas brillig, and the slithy toves
    Did gyre and gimble in the wabe:
All mimsy were the borogoves,
    And the mome raths outgrabe.

"Beware the Jabberwock, my son!
    The jaws that bite, the claws that catch!
Beware the Jubjub bird, and shun
    The frumious Bandersnatch!"

He took his vorpal sword in hand:
    Long time the manxome foe he sought—
So rested he by the Tumtum tree,
    And stood awhile in thought.

And, as in uffish thought he stood,
  The Jabberwock, with eyes of flame,
Came whiffling through the tulgey wood,
  And burbled as it came!

One, two! One, two! And through and through
  The vorpal blade went snicker-snack!
He left it dead, and with its head
  He went galumphing back.

"And hast thou slain the Jabberwock?
  Come to my arms, my beamish boy!
O frabjous day! Callooh! Callay!"
  He chortled in his joy.

'Twas brillig, and the slithy toves
  Did gyre and gimble in the wabe:
All mimsy were the borogoves,
  And the mome raths outgrabe.

The first stanza sets the scene, answering the questions—Who?
What? When? Where? and How. But what exactly are you left with
after you've come to the last word in this stanza? The rest of the poem
tells a story. But in the end, just who has done what to whom?

EXERCISE 4

On a separate page, make a list of the words in the first stanza that
you are unfamiliar with, then look them up in a dictionary and write the
meanings of those that you find beside them. *The Oxford English Dictionary* (OED) will prove the most fruitful here, but if there isn't a copy
at hand, any old thing will do because, you're not going to encounter
very many! Lewis Carroll, the author, made most of them up!
When you're done with the dictionary, go down your list again and
try and guess at the meanings of those words that you did not find. Hint:
it sometimes helps to say them out loud.

After you have finished—and only then—turn this book upside
down for Carroll's explanation of them, as related to Alice by Humpty
Dumpty:

"That'll do very well," said Alice: "and *slithy*?"
begin *broiling* things for dinner."
"*Brillig*, means four o'clock in the afternoon—the time when you

"Well, 'slithy' means 'lithe and slimy.' 'Lithe' is the same as 'active.' You see it's like a portmanteau—there are two meanings packed up into one word."

"I see it now," Alice remarked thoughtfully: "and what are 'toves'?"

"Well, 'toves' are something like badgers—they're something like lizards—and they're something like corkscrews."

"They must be very curious-looking creatures."

"They are that," said Humpty Dumpty: "also they make their nests under sundials—also they live on cheese."

"And what's to 'gyre' and to 'gimble'?"

"To 'gyre' is to go round and round like a gyro-scope. To 'gimble' is to make holes like a gimlet."

"And 'the wabe' is the grass-plot round a sundial, I suppose?" said Alice, surprised at her own ingenuity.

"Of course it is. It's called 'wabe,' you know, because it goes a long way before it, and a long way behind it—"

"And a long way beyond it on each side," Alice added.

"Exactly so. Well then, 'mimsy' is 'flimsy and miserable' (there's another portmanteau for you). And a 'borogove' is a thin shabby-looking bird with its feathers sticking out all round—something like a live mop."

"And then 'mome raths'?" said Alice. "I'm afraid I'm giving you a great deal of trouble."

"Well, a 'rath' is a sort of green pig, but 'mome' I'm not certain about. I think it's short for 'from home'—meaning that they'd lost their way, you know."

"And what does 'outgrabe' mean?"

"Well, 'outgrabing' is something between bellowing and whistling, with a kind of sneeze in the middle: however, you'll hear it done, maybe—down in the wood yonder—and when you've once heard it, you'll be *quite content*."

Crazy, wouldn't you say?

EXERCISE 5

Let's do the same thing with the rest of the words in "Jabberwocky" whose meaning you do not know. Make a list and look them up in your dictionary, then if you don't find them, take an educated guess. Why bother with the dictionary if the author invented them? Well, he didn't invent them all, and some of those that he did, like "chortled," a portmanteau of "chuckle" and "snort," readers of Carroll's time took a fancy to and made a regular part of our language by using, while others the editors of *The Oxford English Dictionary* simply chose to include even though one does not ordinarily employ them in conversation or writing.

Here are the "answers" as culled from Carroll's other writings and correspondence, and those of some of his ingenious explicators, plus a few by yours truly:

Jabberwock—"the result of much excited discussion," a combination of "jabber" and "wocer" or "wocor," the Anglo-Saxon word for "off-spring" or "fruit."

Jubjub—a name. Possibly "jub" is a sound that the bird makes. The *OED* lists *jug* as an imitation of one of the notes of the nightingale.

frumious—a portmanteau of "furious" and "fuming."

Bandersnatch—a name combining "snatch" and "bander," possibly Carroll's diminutive for "band," short for "hairband."

vorpal—possibly a portmanteau of "verbal" and "torpid."

manxome—could be related to Manx, the Celtic name for the Isle of Man.

Tumtum—used to describe the sound of a stringed instrument being monotonously strummed.

uffish—a portmanteau of "gruffish," "roughish," and "huffish."

whiffling—"blowing unsteadily in short puffs."

tulgey—possibly a portmanteau of "bulging" and "turgid."

burbled—a variant of "bubble," also used as a verb meaning "to perplex, confuse, or muddle."

galumphing—a portmanteau of "gallop" and "triumphant."

beamish—a variant of "beaming."

frabjous—very likely a portmanteau of "fabulous" and "joyous."

Callooh—the call of a species of arctic duck so named.

EXERCISE 6

Using your own meanings and/or those above as a key, write a brief summary of what goes on in the poem.

If you are doing these exercises in a class, why not pause here and read your summaries aloud. The best ones will be those that are most clearly stated and at the same time manage to incorporate in some measure Carroll's brand of absurdity.

Enough of Carroll and his nonsense. It's time now to create some that is strictly your own.

EXERCISE 7

In your notebook make a list of the most bizarre and unusual adjectives, nouns, and verbs that you can think of; the more the merrier, so shoot for at least ten of each. Feel free to use the dictionary, and if that doesn't inspire you, flip through another book, like one of your unfavorite textbooks or a newspaper or magazine—or how about your college catalogue. And don't be shy or stuck-up, list all kinds of words—words that sound funny like "pullulate," words that look funny—"coccyx" is a good one—and by all means words out of your own head, including portmanteaus of your own invention.

P.S. If you're unsure of what an adjective, noun, or verb is—don't laugh, you others, it happens—look it up in the dictionary or ask your teacher!

Did you have trouble coming up with ten of each? Well, if you're in a class, lean over and see what your neighbor's been up to. Maybe you can make a deal to swap or borrow one or two. If you're on your own and are stuck, this is a good time to call up a friend.

Be sure to read your lists aloud to one another, and when you do, get your body into the act, express each of your words with actions as well. If you're alone, get hold of that friend again, or if he or she's not available, a pet will do in a pinch—or yourself in the mirror!

EXERCISE 8

In your notebook, create sentences with your crazy words as follows:

1. He _____s the _____ _____.
        verb   adjective   noun

2. Do you want to _____ a _____
              verb   adjective
   _____?
    noun

3. Please don't _____ the _____ _____.
          verb   adjective   noun

4. If the _____ _____ _____s the
     adjective   noun   verb
  _____, then the _____ _____ _____s
   noun   adjective   noun   verb
  the _____ _____.
     adjective   noun

Congratulations! You are now the author of four completely ridiculous sentences and on your way, poetically speaking, but don't ask me where.

Next case.

EXERCISE 9

Imagine two friendly strangers meeting in the dark somewhere. One is an earth person, the other an alien—or else they've both just separately beat it out of a lunatic asylum. Work up a sort of intelligible dialogue between them using words and sentences from the last two exercises and others of your own creation.

Don't neglect to read yours aloud to one another—and do remember your bodies!

Another way of spicing things up verbally is using puns. Only for this you have to use your head, so if yours is tucked away somewhere, like under a wing, get it out.

Did you know that there is more than one kind of pun, three to be exact? They all have ghastly names like diseases, but what they stand for is fairly straightforward:

> *paranomasia*—using two or more words that sound alike. Example: The prophets prophesied by Baal and walked after the things that do not profit.
> *antanaclasis*—using the same word in two or more senses. Example: There are three ways to waylay someone.
> *syllepsis*—using the same word literally and figuratively. Example: The jilted girl ate her sandwich and her heart out.

EXERCISE 10

> Try using all three kinds of puns together in one blast. Did you think that you were going to get away easily? No such luck. Sometimes this works better if written in the form of a brief note to a friend. Isn't there someone whom you owe a letter to? If there isn't, pretend that you do.
> Psst! If you feel that you need a crutch, use the words from the examples above.

EXERCISE 11

> Do the same thing, but this time definitely with your own words.

CRAZY WORLDS

The real world is crazy enough without adding to it, you might be saying. Okay, but a created one need not be bad—can in fact be quite lovely and awesome, as that presented by Samuel Taylor Coleridge in his "Kubla Khan":

In Xanadu did Kubla Khan
A stately pleasure-dome decree:
Where Alph, the sacred river, ran
Through caverns measureless to man
   Down to a sunless sea.
So twice five miles of fertile ground
   With walls and towers were girdled round:
And there were gardens bright with sinuous rills,
Where blossomed many an incense-bearing tree;
And here were forests ancient as the hills,
Enfolding sunny spots of greenery.

But oh! that deep romantic chasm which slanted
Down the green hill athwart a cedarn cover!
A savage place! as holy and enchanted
As e'er beneath a waning moon was haunted
By woman wailing for her demon-lover!
And from this chasm, with ceaseless turmoil seething,
As if this earth in fast thick pants were breathing,
A mighty fountain momently was forced:
Amid whose swift half-intermitted burst
Huge fragments vaulted like rebounding hail,
Or chaffy grain beneath the thresher's flail:
And 'mid these dancing rocks at once and ever
It flung up momently the sacred river.
Five miles meandering with a mazy motion
Through wood and dale the sacred river ran,
Then reached the caverns measureless to man,
And sank in tumult to a lifeless ocean:
And 'mid this tumult Kubla heard from far
Ancestral voices prophesying war!
   The shadow of the dome of pleasure
   Floated midway on the waves;
   Where was heard the mingled measure
   From the fountain and the caves.
It was a miracle of rare device,
A sunny pleasure-dome with caves of ice!

"Miracle of rare device" could well be used to describe Coleridge's rendering of this vision too, don't you agree?

But what makes the world of "Kubla Khan" so strange? It's not the dome and its environs; they're too regular and pretty. Nor is it the chasm and surrounding terrain, awesome and frightening though they might be—it's a familiar enough scene to one living in the temperate zone at least. No, the strangeness comes from the scenes of repose and turbulence being in the neighborhood of one another, as summed up in the line, "a sunny pleasure-dome with caves of ice." For how can ice last like that in the warm sun without melting, and what's a dome intended for good times doing in proximity to such coldness, br-r-r?

EXERCISE 12

How would one conclude such a vision? Take a whack at it, imitating the verse form, or suggest an appropriate finale in a paragraph or two of prose.

Note: If you really like "Kubla Khan" and feel that you would be desecrating it by doing the above, let it be and turn this book around to see how the master handled it.

And drunk the milk of Paradise.
For he on honey-dew hath fed,
And close your eyes with holy dread,
Weave a circle round him thrice,
His flashing eyes, his floating hair!
And all should cry, Beware! Beware!
And all who heard should see them there,
That sunny dome! those caves of ice!
I would build that dome in air,
That with music loud and long,
To such a deep delight 'twould win me,
Her symphony and song,
Could I revive within me
Singing of Mount Abora.
And on her dulcimer she played,
It was an Abyssinian maid,
In a vision once I saw:
A damsel with a dulcimer

Breathtaking, isn't it? . . .
It's do-it-yourself time.

EXERCISE 13

Make a list of ten or so adjectives, nouns, and verbs that you might use to create your own strange world. Notice that those Coleridge employed to achieve his effects, like "sunny," are quite ordinary by anybody's standards. So this time try and select much the same.

Have a general discussion of your different crazy worlds, or if you're working by yourself, make notes.

EXERCISE 14

Get busy. Create your world any old way, preferably as a poem, but if you don't feel up to that yet, do it in prose or even dialogue form.

The rest is silence. (Who said that?)

CHAPTER TWO
Style ? ! ?

It is sometimes said that a poet's audience is him- or herself; readers are subsequent eavesdroppers. Just how does one relate to oneself and beyond to one's audience with words and the attitude or tone they convey? Whether you are a beginning poet or seasoned veteran reconsidering what you have been doing, this is probably one of the first things that occurred to you after going through the previous chapter. If not, then it certainly has now.

THE TRADITIONAL CHOICES: FORMAL, INFORMAL, COLLOQUIAL

In the good old days before the student revolution in the late 1960's, three levels of style were recognized in literary circles no matter what the kind of writing—formal, informal and colloquial. While these distinctions are largely passé nowadays except in some bastions of conservatism, a closer look at them may prove helpful as a preliminary step in defining yourself as a poet. Formal, characterized by long, complicated sentences, a sophisticated vocabulary that avoided contractions like "isn't" and other abbreviations, and strict adherence to grammatical rule, such as maintaining the distinction between "that" and "which," was mandatory for very serious situations, such as a learned discourse. Colloquial, where one used predominantly simple sentences involving a limited vocabulary generously sprinkled with slang, and a loose grammatical structure, was reserved for personal situations like a letter to a close friend. Informal obviously fell between these two stools.

Let the following passage from philosopher George Santayana's *The Sense of Beauty*, written in a formal style, together with informal and colloquial renderings serve as an example:

Formal

There are, indeed, other objects of desire that if attained leave nothing but restlessness and dissatisfaction behind them. These are the objects pursued by fools. That such objects ever attract us is a proof of the disorganization of our nature, which drives us in contrary directions and is at war with itself. If we had attained anything like steadiness of thought or fixity of character, if we knew ourselves, we should know also our inalienable satisfactions.

Informal

We all have foolish desires. We want things which do not satisfy us when we get them. We are subject to conflicting desires and want to go in opposite directions at the same time. If we had a clearer understanding of our own needs and purposes, we would know what course was best for us.

Colloquial

We all have dumb ideas. The things we want we don't go for once we get them. We're full of urges, and they don't agree with one another. If we knew what was ailing us, everything would be okay.

EXERCISE 1

Analyze Santayana's paragraph and the two renderings according to the criteria given above.

The differences in vocabulary alone are telling, but I hope that you noticed those of sentence length and complexity as well.

EXERCISE 2

The following words and phrases are of an informal nature—poetically we might say that they are colorless: make love, old man, old woman, small, shoot, girl, husband, businessman, beautiful, ugly, shy, amusing, dead man, dog, kiss, wife, cigarette, flower. See if you can supply formal and colloquial synonyms for them. If you run into difficulty, consult a dictionary or, better yet, a thesaurus (synonym word book) if you have one. (If you don't, consider acquiring one—soon.)

No use giving the answers to this because they're in the dictionary. So if you didn't find them, keep looking.

EXERCISE 3

The following is from Irwin Edman's *Arts and the Man*:

To the more disciplined musical intelligence, music may come to be more than a pyrotechnic attack upon the eardrum, a splendid fireworks of sound. There is perhaps no other art where the pleasures of mere form are more marvelous in complexity, more intellectual in essence, in qual-

ity more pure. The complication of musical structure is indeed express-
ible only in music itself, for neither language nor life permits such
involution and internal reticulation as is possible in those edifices, tran-
siently existing in time, that we call musical compositions.

Make translations of it into "informalese" and "colloquialese." By all
means feel free to look words up in your dictionary and thesaurus—after
all, that's what they're for.

Be sure to read the passage and your creations aloud to one another
when you're done, or again, if you're alone, practice in the mirror.
Don't hesitate to adopt the appropriate facial expression and body pose.

EXERCISE 4

There used to be a popular song that began, "I got along withoutcha
before I metcha, gonna get along withoutcha now." See if you can come
up with formal and informal versions of it.

If you're unaccustomed to using long words and fancy phrases, don't
be upset if other folks find your formalese comical when you didn't
intend it to be. It's a little like trying on mom's high heels or dad's pants
when you were a kid. Sooner or later you'll get the hang of it, just as
you didn't fit into the heels or pants then.

Now that you understand what formal, informal, and colloquial levels of style mean, let's take a look at two poetic illustrations. Consider
the opening to T. S. Eliot's "The Love Song of J. Alfred Prufrock,"
where the "I" invites us to go out for a walk into the city at dusk with
him. The language alone is enough to show us that the style is a formal
one. Find a copy of the poem in any standard anthology and note that
fact if you haven't—note learned words and phrases like "etherised,"
"tedious argument," "insidious intent," and "overwhelming question."
If you read on in the poem, you will see that such formality is in keeping
with Prufrock's reserved character—but if you then turn to Eliot's other
works, you will soon realize, if you haven't already, that his style
generally conforms to that above. Eliot's intention in "Prufrock" and
elsewhere would seem to have been to lead the reader along, but at a
distance.

Our other example is Emily Dickinson's well-known, "I Heard a Fly
Buzz":

I heard a Fly buzz—when I died—
The Stillness in the Room
Was like the Stillness in the Air—
Between the Heaves of Storm—

The Eyes around—had wrung them dry—
And Breaths were gathering firm
For that last Onset—when the King
Be witnessed—in the Room—

I willed my Keepsakes—Signed away
What portion of me be
Assignable—and then it was
There interposed a Fly—

With Blue—uncertain stumbling Buzz—
Between the light—and me—
And then the Windows failed—and then
I could not see to see—

The contrast with Eliot stylistically should be apparent at once—the language simple, though not simple-minded, the appeal direct.

So where do you as a poet or budding poet fit in? Do you lean or want to lean on Eliot's side or is your penchant more toward Emily Dickinson? Let's see if we can find an answer for right now. Bear in mind this may not be where you end up.

EXERCISE 5

Take one of your poems, or something else of suitable length and substance that you've written in your notebook. A completed exercise from the last chapter will do. Analyze it stylistically, considering the vocabulary and phrasing including sentence length and structure if there are sentences, as you did before with the selection from Santayana. This may prove a bit more than you want to bite off right now—some students liken it to a surgeon trying to operate on him- or herself. If that turns out to be the case, exchange with some neighbor, keeping in mind that you're both in the same boat.

So where are you right now? Does your piece seem to fall under one heading, and if it does, which one is that—formal, informal, or colloquial? Don't be surprised—or alarmed—if you find that it's in a category all by itself, combining features of one, two, or all three levels of style.

More important, whatever the analysis shows, is this how you want to present yourself to yourself and to readers?

If not, fine, it's time for a change.

Even if you are content with your style as it is, it will not be amiss
to follow along here. You may end up wanting to do a little refining.

So how do you do it? How do you find yourself stylistically if you
don't really have a style or are dissatisfied with the one you have
discovered? The answer is, purely and simply, by mulling things over.
How do you look at yourself? How do you look at the rest of the world?
And yet it's not mulling either—it's more like getting a sense of things.

Sometimes it helps to take a long walk. Try it if you're of a peram-
bulating bent. But if you do, take your time—I mean go slow—so that
your mental processes can work unimpeded by the hard breathing and
muscle fatigue that come with strenuous physical exertion. A painter at
an art colony that I went to recently once remarked that you can always
tell a poet from a distance because poets stroll, everyone else—
including novelists, composers, and painters like himself—always seems
to be in a terrible rush. So do just that, be a poet even if you have
certain doubts about yourself right now, stroll.   Here is the result of
one such jaunt or a series of jaunts outdoors by contemporary poet
Colette Inez, entitled "Skokie River Cadenzas":

1
Dazed, a birch leaf sails downstream
out of the hubbub of hornets and bees
raiding the field.
Here, where the river slows its course,
I watch the print of a snail's back
repeat in spirals of water.

2
In slowmotion, my body turns
through a keyhole of light
out of the forest and into the meadow.
Springtails and mites
seem to study angles of light on moss
like geometers.
In a margin of grass, a cricket stops
to revise its ancient argument.

3
Its back scored with six black notes
on an orange field, the beetle clings
in a curled up nest of Queen Anne's lace.
Rippling hours in waves, the day
embraces dragonflies and wasps, a katydid
skipping a beat on its narrow scale,
a finch's wing skimming the thistle.

4
From distant cornrows, a lone crow calls.
Drugged on goldenrod and vervain, the field
lies open mouthed in a dream.
Drowsy, I stumble on the river's branch,
a languorous stream, but when I turn
my back, the sassafras tree jolts into gold,
the red oak, brown.

5
What is to come sleeps in the bud
now tilting upwards towards a thinning light.
Later, as I trace the path, the river passes
out of sight.

There's no need to say another word about it, is there? It's all there
in those final lines, "What is to come sleeps in the bud" and "the river
passes out of sight."

Sometimes when you're walking, the mind turns inward and you
begin thinking of something else. In "Honorable Discharge," another
contemporary poet, Walter James Miller, strolled back into the past,
when he was in the U.S. Army, and at the same time made a comment
about how we humans—indeed, even the poets among us—number,
weigh, and measure ourselves:

Naked in February	in a line of blue veterans
I step onto	a snowcold scale
A medic warm in shoes	and white uniform
Swings a horizontal rod	scrapes my scalp
Calls out	70½"
Indifferent a clerk scribbles it into my discharge papers	

Shocked again	by war's paradox
I fade back into	1083
Mornings before when	I shivered

Naked in February   on a line of
blue recruits and   didn't the military
Statistic me then   as 72″ high?

How can a man lose   so much stature
During such a meaningless   parenthesis?

Maybe, standing indignant   a man is his tallest?
Crouching to run   he lowers himself?

1083   days and nights
in olive drab   in camouflage
Army Serial Number   32812510(h)
Officially pronounced   as ending in zero

Marching deluded   by anti-fascist music
In corrugated ranks   of a fascist army
Marching muted into   1083
Blurred sunsets   *Eyes—right!*
Braincase shrinking   ears antennaed from
Listening asleep   lungs shrunk from
Answering back only   beneath my breath
Shrunken brainpower   settling down on
Collapsing lungpower

                        Crouching to run
I grunt gratitude   that I'm pinched
And stunted only   1½″

But once I thrust   a happy foot
Through trousers   of my own choosing
Landscape my mane   into my own shape
Once I spark new synapses   from heart's hot candor
Gallop fiercely through   to love's languor
Then I shall answer   10,830
Precise sunrises   taller than ruler can measure

In her rambles one day, Ruth Fainlight conjured up this lively picture of herself and her late mother in "Love-Feast":

Sulphur-yellow mushrooms like unlaid, unshelled eggs
inside a chicken's stomach when my mother cleaned it.
This morning, mushrooms on the lawn made me remember.

Bright as dew on the grass and silver with air-bubbles,
a stream of water splashed from the dull brass tap against
the side of the sink and over her red-chilled fingers when she
opened the carcass and laughed to show me how some were almost
ready—yolks only needing their coating of lime and mucus,
while others were still half-formed, small as pearls or seeds.

Always, once the chicken was plucked and quartered and boiling,
my mother would take those eggs, marked with twisting coils of
crimson threads like bloodshot eyes, and the liver put aside
on the draining-board in a chipped old china saucer, and fry them
with an onion to make our private treat. In the steamy
kitchen, the two of us would eat, and love each other.

Notice how the sight of the mushrooms made the poet remember the eggs, and then the rest of the scene came.

Strolls are best taken alone, but if you have a friend—a special friend who is a poet—with whom you'd like to share your walks, that's all right too. The composition of poetry, in fact, is a very lonely activity, as perhaps you've already discovered, but there have been and can be exceptions. For instance, the English Romantic poets Wordsworth and Coleridge hiked together and composed in their heads as they trudged along, and the fruits were even published together in *The Lyrical Ballads*, which included Wordsworth's celebrated "Tintern Abbey" and Coleridge's "Rime of the Ancient Mariner."

If you're unable to get around much or are not fond of it, try sitting or lying somewhere—my own favorite position is on my back staring up at the ceiling with arms behind my head. But whatever you do, make sure that your roost is quiet—even if you are of the opinion that you function well with background noise. Think of insulating yourself, of peace and quiet as equivalent to the spacesuit an astronaut wears.

Sometimes reading poems by others helps, and for this you should have at least an anthology. Look at the list at the end of this book and take your pick, and then when you acquire it, browse through it as you would through a bookstore, reading snatches here and there until something catches your attention. Then make yourself nice and comfortable and stick with it.

If one poet in particular begins to interest you, go on to other poems by him or her, and if you really take a fancy or find yourself identifying with it, obtain a complete volume of his or her works if such a thing exists. Remember your library; if your bookstore tells you that such a work is not in print, the library might have a copy, or will probably be able to borrow one for you from somewhere else.

One thing I must caution against, though, is confining yourself to living poets and the present—don't lose touch with the past. So when it comes to investing in that anthology, you might want to think about getting two, one of contemporary poetry and another offering a general survey.

Besides poetry, don't forget the many great writers of lyrical prose, especially those of the recent past like Thomas Wolfe and Marcel Proust. Dip into them in the same way that you would the poets. Read a little, read some more. You might even take a little peek into a "poetical" something called *Klytaimnestra Who Stayed at Home* by yours truly.

EXERCISE 6

When you are done with wool-gathering, whether it be on your back, in a chair, or in the outdoors, take your pen and notebook and write, just write—any old thing in any old way. Keep at it until you feel truly drained, as if you were in need of a nap, which may very well be so.

When you're finished, nap or no, set your jottings—the fruits—aside and go on about your business, allowing at least twenty-four hours to pass before you take them up again.

Now what say you? Does the self that they reveal—the poetic self, if you will—square with the image of yourself as poet that you were left with at the end of Exercise 5? If so, congratulations on your early arrival. If not, congratulations are also in order, on unearthing the new—the real!—you. On the other hand, if you haven't gotten off the ground with any of this, don't despair. Forget about your poetic identity for the time being and go on with the book and course if you're taking one—return to this chapter later by yourself . . . deliciously by yourself.

CHAPTER THREE
Some useful aids and tools

Finding yourself as a poet is not the whole answer. On the contrary, you've really just begun, for being a poet requires a knowledge of a craft, and being adept with certain tools and skills.

Many of the things that one uses in writing prose—good prose, that is—can likewise be used for composing poetry, above all the metaphor and closely related simile. A poet should also be able to describe both what a person, place, or thing looks like and how it acts. There are many other handy tools that one should be familiar with, which I've lumped together in a grab bag—including a group titled quaint curiosities.

METAPHORICALLY SPEAKING

Human language is by its nature metaphorical. No matter what culture we come from, we employ metaphors every day of our lives in every way. "What a jackass I am!" "Where did the time go?" These are both examples of our daily metaphor usage. Nor do we have a finite number of metaphors; everyone is constantly coming up with new ones, just as new forms of life are forever being evolved here on our Earth.

What exactly is a metaphor, you may be asking. Well, let's call it an identification of a person, place, or thing with something else in order to elucidate or cast some new light on that person, place, or thing. For instance, in the common everyday examples above, the "I" is equating him or herself with a jackass and time is being viewed as something capable of movement, like a train.

EXERCISE 1

Try your hand at creating a few metaphors. If you get stuck, opt for something you've heard someone say recently.

There are two secrets to good metaphor writing. One's reader should find it easy to re-create your identification in his or her mind, meaning that the something else must be familiar to most people; certainly a jackass and a mobile entity are. At the same time, that something should be attention-getting, providing readers with a new dimension or insight into the thing being identified—which is not exactly the case with the "I" as jackass and time as something that moves.

William Blake's "London" is chock full of metaphors, all of them still as fresh as on the day he wrote them:

I wander thro' each charter'd street,
Near where the charter'd Thames does flow,
And mark in every face I meet
Marks of weakness, marks of woe.

In every cry of every Man,
In every Infant's cry of fear,
In every voice, in every ban,
The mind-forg'd manacles I hear.

How the Chimney-sweeper's cry
Every black'ning Church appalls;
And the hapless Soldier's sigh
Runs in blood down Palace walls.

But most thro' midnight streets I hear
How the youthful Harlot's curse
Blasts the new born Infant's tear,
And blights with plagues the Marriage hearse.

In the first two stanzas everything makes sense, there's a logical order to the "I" 's ideas—he wanders, and as he does so, he sees and hears. And as you very likely noticed, Blake began very simply, with very simple metaphors—indeed corresponding to someone setting off on a walk. "Chartered" refers to the *Magna Carta*, which granted every Englishman certain rights and privileges, and is here a negative, Blake having believed that all men are born with those rights, like so many advanced thinkers of his day. His position becomes clear with "mind-forg'd manacles" or thought control, a relatively new idea in the late eighteenth century. These manacles are "heard" in men's and children's voices, a further metaphorical complication—normally a prisoner shakes real chains in a real prison.

From here on the metaphors begin coming thick and fast, and at the same time are increasingly dense—as if the "I" had quickened his pace. Indeed so thorny do they become that it would take many pages to explore, so let's just touch on the highlights. In the third stanza, black

and red, the colors of Church and State, predominate, and there are
more alarming sights and sounds of woe yet. The cry of the Chimney-
sweeper, himself begrimed by the work that society forces him to do,
appalls (a negatively blackening word) an already smoke-begritted
church. The sigh of the Soldier, in red coat and apparently wounded,
runs in blood down Palace walls. In the final stanza the young Harlot's
curse blights and blasts, but the plague is venereal disease. Further, the
targets of her "curse" are infants and marriage instead of the crops
traditionally withered by blight by the deity worshipped in the Church.
And to go even further, marriage, itself a detestable priest-ridden in-
stitution, is a hearse or kind of death.

EXERCISE 2

It is difficult even conceiving of following such a class act, but let's
try. Get hold of a subject, let's say, love-making. Try to create a chain of
metaphors with respect to it in the manner of Blake. Do it in prose so
that you can devote your full attention to it.

As we have seen with Blake's "London," metaphors can range from
being quite simple to highly complex. Indeed, quite a number of experts have been at pains to write about metaphors, and for a good
capsule sketch, may I recommend the section dealing with them in
William Packard's *The Poet's Dictionary*. One thing only would I im-
press upon new or reconsidering poets here is that metaphors must
come of themselves, just as poems must. Never force one; never say,
"My poem is too plain, I have to put some metaphors into it," or
something like that. Better to let it be.

Besides being complicated, metaphors can also be long, in which
case they are called extended metaphors. The whole of Blake's "Garden
of Love" is such:

I went to the Garden of Love,
And saw what I never had seen:
A Chapel was built in the midst,
Where I used to play on the green.

And the gates of this Chapel were shut,
And "Thou shalt not" writ over the door;
So I turn'd to the Garden of Love,
That so many sweet flowers bore,

And I saw it was filled with graves,
And tomb-stones where flowers should be;
And Priests in black gowns were walking their rounds,
And binding with briars my joys & desires.

What happens here is pure and simple. To paraphrase: I went to see someone I deeply cared for, who I assumed cared as much for me, only to discover that she had become falsely religious, smothering her true feelings with mindless pious observances.

Not only whole poems, but also long works both in verse and prose, occupying many hundreds of pages, can be construed as metaphors. For instance, Chaucer's *Canterbury Tales* is in one sense the story of a soul on the road to fulfillment or redemption.

EXERCISE 4

Choose one of your metaphors from the two previous exercises and develop it further, making the thing identified more explicit and striking.

Something remains to be said about mixed metaphors. When I was a wee child in public school, the teachers were always after us to avoid using them—"the lights screamed" and such like. But in college, I discovered that mixing metaphors was an old literary trick of the trade. Consider Hamlet's debating whether or not to "take arms against a sea of troubles" in "To Be or Not To Be." Who shoots at or duels with the ocean, or with one's troubles for that matter? And consider Milton's railing against the gold-grasping clergy of his time as "blind mouths" in his poem "Lycidas," when of course he thought of them as possessing "hungry" or "greedy" mouths and being spiritually blind. The trick is in mixing metaphors effectively, as they did.

EXERCISE 5

Let's see if you can do better than the following: the soapy cat barked up a storm of protest.

What's a simile for?

As the look and sound of the word imply, a simile is a comparison, and a metaphor, as I learned it, is a compressed simile—that is, a simile minus the comparing word "like" or "as." But we don't use similes nearly as much, so let's say rather that they are specialized forms of metaphor. Specifically they are comparisons—electrifying comparisons—between two unlike things, again for the sake of elucidating or casting light.

"Jane eats like a bird" and "Jack is as slow as molasses in the morning" are as good examples as any from our daily lives. But in the hands of a master, similes can add a certain finishing touch to a work. Note, for instance, how well similes serve Herman Melville in this passage from *Moby Dick*:

> Next morning the not-yet-subsided sea rolled in long slow billows of mighty bulk, and striving in the Pequod's gurgling track, pushed her on *like giants' palms outstretched*. The strong, unstaggering breeze abounded so, that *sky and air seemed vast outbellying sails*; the whole world boomed before the wind. Muffled in the full morning light, the invisible sun was only known by the spread intensity of his place; where his bayonet rays moved on in stacks. Emblazonings, as of crowned Babylonian kings and queens, reigned over everything. The sea was *as a crucible of molten gold, that bubblingly leaps with light and heat.*

How diminished this passage would be without those similes.

EXERCISE 6

Don't just agree—or disagree. Demonstrate this for yourself. Read the passage aloud as is, then read it again without the similes, running on "the strong unstaggering breeze abounded so" with "that the whole world boomed before the wind," and changing the last sentence to "The sea was bubbling with light and heat."

If you still don't agree that the similes make a real difference—some people won't—best discuss it with others.

No matter how one relates them to each other, metaphors and similes rarely translate well into one another. To illustrate with our clichés—"How like a jackass I am!" lacks the pizzazz of "What a jackass I am," and the same can be said of Jane and her anorectic tendencies—"Jane eats like a bird" has far more punch to it than "Jane is a bird when it comes to eating."

Needless to say, the secret of writing good similes is the same as that for writing good metaphors. The term of comparison should be unusual, but at the same time it has to be recognizable.

EXERCISE 7

Take some piece you've written and add a simile or two to it. If you run into trouble, by all means try it the quick and dirty way by doctoring an already existing metaphor, but beware of what I have said about their untranslatability.

It's possible to achieve an effect by stringing similes together. Here is a really way-out example from the Song of Songs in the Bible, which

some experts believe to be a collection of ancient courtship and wed-
ding songs. First a "he" sings, then a while later, a "she":

> BEHOLD, thou art fair, my love; behold, thou art fair; thou hast
> doves' eyes within thy locks: thy hair is as a flock of goats, that appear
> from mount Gilead.
> Thy teeth are like a flock of sheep that are even shorn, which came up
> from the washing; whereof every one bear twins, and none is barren
> among them.
> Thy lips are like a thread of scarlet, and thy speech is comely: thy
> temples are like a piece of pomegranate within thy locks.
> Thy neck is like the tower of David builded for an armoury, whereon
> there hang a thousand bucklers, all shields of mighty men.
> Thy two breasts are like two young roes that are twins, which feed
> among the lilies. . . .

> My beloved is white and ruddy, the chiefest among ten thousand.
> His head is as the most fine gold, his locks are bushy, and black as a
> raven.
> His eyes are as the eyes of doves by the rivers of waters, washed with
> milk, and fitly set.
> His cheeks are as a bed of spices, as sweet flowers: his lips like lilies,
> dropping sweet smelling myrrh.
> His hands are as gold rings set with the beryl: his belly is as bright
> ivory overlaid with sapphires.
> His legs are as pillars of marble, set upon sockets of fine gold: his
> countenance is as Lebanon, excellent as the cedars.
> His mouth is most sweet: yea, he is altogether lovely. This is my
> beloved, and this is my friend, O daughters of Jerusalem.

Overdone these similes are, there is no question about it. But they do
help to convey a general feeling of lushness and eroticism, which seems
to have been the author's or authors' intention.

EXERCISE 8

> Think of someone to whom you are attracted and make a list of his or
> her attributes that are particularly appealing. Just for fun, attach a simile
> to each. If you're in a class, bear in mind that you may have to read
> yours aloud—that, or come to an understanding with your instructor
> beforehand that students if they wish can skip their turn when called
> upon.

Just as with metaphors there are long versions of similes, one coming
to us from the Bible, others from Homer's *Iliad* and *Odyssey*, which
relate stories of the Trojan War and its aftermath. The biblical extended simile, known as a parable, was used as a teaching device to a

receptive, non-reading public. Something (A) is compared to something else (B), and then that something else (B) is elaborated upon with the idea that the person instructed will apply it to the original something (A). Jesus's celebrated Parable of the Mustard Seed will make this clearer:

> Another parable put he forth unto them, saying, The kingdom of heaven is like to a grain of mustard seed, which a man took, and sowed in his field:
>
> Which indeed is the least of all seeds: but when it is grown, it is the greatest among herbs, and becometh a tree, so that the birds of the air come and lodge in the branches thereof.

It is understood that the birds of the air are us, humanity.

EXERCISE 9

> More for the sake of your lingering in the simile vein rather than from any utilitarian motive, may I suggest that you try your hand at a parable yourself. If you find yourself casting about for a subject, use "life" and begin with something, say, like "Life is like a flower garden."

Homer's extended similes are known as epic similes, and were used to clarify a specific event involving action and the emotion aroused by it. In this selection from *The Iliad*, the setting is the beach near the plain of Troy, where the Greek besiegers have their ships anchored. Hektor, leader of the Trojan army, has launched a counter-attack against them. Among the Greeks is Telemonian Aias, who is spoiling for a fight with the champion on the one hand, but on the other is worried about the real danger to the fleet. So he views Hektor's approach with longing and apprehension, and his state of mind is compared to that of a lion being kept at bay from some cattle by a bunch of men:

> He stood stunned, and swung the sevenfold ox-hide shield behind him
> and drew back, throwing his eyes round the crowd of men, like a wild
>   beast,
> turning on his way, shifting knee past knee only a little;
> as when the men who live in the wild and their dogs have driven
> a tawny lion away from the mid-fenced ground of their oxen,
> and will not let him tear out the fat of the oxen, watching
> nightlong against him, and he in his hunger for meat closes in
> but can get nothing of what he wants, for the raining javelins

> thrown from the daring hands of the men beat ever against him,
> and the flaming torches, and these he balks at for all of his fury
> and with the daylight goes away, disappointed of desire;
> so Aias, disappointed at heart, drew back from the Trojans
> much unwilling, but feared for the ships of the Achaians.

Extended similes of this variety served as models for all future writers of epic, from Virgil in his *Aeneid*, the story of the escape of Aeneas from Troy to Italy and subsequent founding of Rome by his descendants, to Milton in his thoroughly Christian treatment of the Fall in *Paradise Lost*, and beyond to Wordsworth's poetical autobiography, *The Prelude*.

EXERCISE 10

What have you got to lose? Try your hand at an epic simile too. Using as a departure point some event in sports like a baseball player stealing a base or some popular performer on TV often yields interesting results.

DESCRIBING

The workhorse of description so far as appearances are concerned is the adjective. Consider how bare or flat this statement is without one:

The man looked at his watch.

Now look at what happens when two quite ordinary adjectives are added:

The old man looked at his gold watch.

Our mental image is sharpened; it's almost as if we had fine-tuned a picture through a camera lens before taking it. Yes, adjectives are truly invaluable when it comes to describing what someone or something is like—they are the jewels of verbal adornment.

EXERCISE 11

Think up another adjective with which to describe the man's watch. If you're using this book by yourself, provide more than one.

These should definitely be read aloud, and when they are, notice how many different pictures of the watch you get just because of that one word-change.

Now that you have gotten your feet wet, here are a few rules of thumb to remember when using adjectives. Never overuse them unless a situation calls for it; bear in mind what someone looks like when he or she is overloaded with jewelry. Another thing, avoid commonly-used adjectives like "beautiful," "gorgeous," "swell," "great," and so on, which are so worked-to-death they tell very little and so are utterly non-descriptive! Try each of these "old shoes" with "watch" to see what I mean.

Adjectives are not the only parts of speech that one can use to describe appearances. Nouns themselves can also be employed toward that end, and better yet, nouns in combination with adjectives. Note our model now:

The elderly gentleman looked at his rare, gold timepiece.

Note it again:

The old geezer looked at his tarnished ticktock.

Some difference, wouldn't you say?

EXERCISE 12

Using adjectives and nouns of your own choosing, work up your own distinctive picture of a person looking at a watch. If it suits you, change the age and/or gender of your subject.

That would seem to be the end of describing people and things, but not so. Verbs too can be enlisted to serve in that cause. For example, the verb "look" in our models is rather neutral. When something more appropriate to the individual is substituted in each case, the pictures solidify—they become complete:

The elderly gentleman consulted his rare, gold timepiece.
The old geezer peered at his tarnished ticktock.

EXERCISE 13

Return to your sentence in the previous exercise and try out different verbs until you fasten on one that is ideal. Here is an occasion when you might want to go to a thesaurus or dictionary that supplies synonyms.

Now let's see an example of describing appearances from the world of "reality." The following passage is from a short story entitled "Ligeia" by Edgar Allan Poe, who, if you recall, was the author of the celebrated poem "The Raven." Ligeia is the name of the heroine of this story, and Poe describes her eyes, an all-important feature, because she dies and returns from the dead at the end of the story and it's her eyes that one principally sees then.

Read this piece over to yourself, but to do it justice, someone ought to read it aloud after.

For eyes we have no models in the remotely antique. It might have been, too, that in these eyes of my beloved lay the secret to which Lord Verulam alludes. They were, I must believe, far larger than the ordinary eyes of our own race. They were even fuller than the fullest of the gazelle eyes of the tribe of the valley of Nourjahad. Yet it was only at intervals—in moments of intense excitement—that this peculiarity became more than slightly noticeable in Ligeia. And at such moments was her beauty—in my heated fancy thus it appeared perhaps—the beauty of beings either above or apart from the earth—the beauty of the fabulous Houri of the Turk. The hue of the orbs was the most brilliant of black, and, far over them, hung jetty lashes of great length. The brows, slightly irregular in outline, had the same tint. The "strangeness," however, which I found in the eyes was of a nature distinct from the formation, or the color, or the brilliancy of the features, and must, after all, be referred to the *expression*. Ah, word of no meaning! behind whose vast latitude of mere sound we intrench our ignorance of so much of the spiritual. The expression of the eyes of Ligeia! How for long hours have I pondered upon it! How have I, through the whole of a midsummer night, struggled to fathom it! What was it—that something more profound than the well of Democritus—which lay far within the pupils of my beloved? What *was* it? I was possessed with a passion to discover. Those eyes! those large, those shining, those divine orbs! they became to me twin stars of Leda, and I to them devoutest of astrologers.

There is no point, among the many incomprehensible anomalies of the science of mind, more thrillingly exciting than the fact—never, I believe, noticed in the schools—that in our endeavors to recall to memory something long forgotten, we often find ourselves *upon the very verge* of remembrance, without being able, in the end, to remember. And thus how frequently, in my intense scrutiny of Ligeia's eyes, have I felt approaching the full knowledge of their expression—felt it approaching—yet not quite be mine—and so at length entirely depart! And (strange, oh, strangest mystery of all!) I found, in the commonest objects of the universe, a circle of analogies to that expression. I mean to say that, subsequently to the period when Ligeia's beauty passed into my spirit, there dwelling as in a shrine, I derived, from many existences in the material world, a sentiment such as I felt always around, within me, by her large and luminous orbs. Yet not the more could I define that sentiment, or analyze, or even steadily view it. I recognize it, let me repeat, sometimes in the survey of a rapidly growing vine—in the contemplation of a moth, a butterfly, a chrysalis, a stream of running water. I have felt it in the ocean—in the falling of a meteor. I have felt it in the glances of unusually aged people. And there are one or two stars in heaven (one especially, a star of the sixth magnitude, double and changeable, to be found near the large star in Lyra) in a telescopic scrutiny of which I have been made aware of the feeling. I have been filled with it by certain sounds from stringed instruments, and not unfrequently by passages from books. Among innumerable other instances, I well remember something in a volume of Joseph Glanvill, which (perhaps merely from its quaintness—who shall say?) never failed to inspire me with the sentiment: "And the will therein lieth, which dieth not. Who knoweth the mysteries of the will, with its vigor? For God is but a great will pervading all things by nature of its intentness. Man doth not yield him to the angels, nor unto death utterly, save only through the weakness of his feeble will."

Wild, isn't it? Did you ever know of a person to carry on so about someone's eyes?

EXERCISE 14

Make a list of adjectives, nouns, and verbs that Poe used in this passage. Be sure to include allusions like the "twin stars of Leda."

Another discussion might be in order here, followed if possible by another reading of this passage aloud.

EXERCISE 15

Think of someone you know who has memorable eyes, or take a good look at yourself in the mirror—and get to work.

Don't worry if things did not come out as well as you would have liked them to. Good description takes a lot of practice.

Describing actions involves verbs first and foremost, obviously. Here is another bland sentence:

The man threw the ball.

Threw is the key word here, without which we would have a considerably diminished mental picture. Substituting a more specific synonym for it—say, to *flung, tossed, hurled,* or *lofted*—not only changes the way the ball sails through the air but also the stance and arm movements of the person releasing it.

But, while finding more specific verbs may be the first order of the day when it comes to describing action, it is not the only one. Showing how a person or thing looks while in the act also adds to the picture—in other words doing the same thing as we did above when describing appearances. Notice, for instance, what happens to our model when we add an adjective or substitute a new set of nouns with modifiers:

The decrepit old man lofted the ball.
The little girl in the pretty pink dress lofted the ball.

And adding a few more brush strokes to the thing acted upon, in this case the ball, clarifies things even further:

The decrepit old man lofted the brand-new soccer ball.
The little girl in the pretty pink dress lofted the mud-bespattered tennis ball.

Is that all there is to describing action? By no means. Just as persons, places, and things can be given more definiteness by adjectives, so too can verbs be "fleshed out" by adverbs. In the case of our examples, such a verbal modifier truly completes the picture:

The decrepit old man painfully lofted the brand-new soccer ball.
The little girl in the pretty pink dress carelessly lofted the mud-bespattered tennis ball.

Not only do we see in our minds a clearly delineated action, we are also inclined to suspect a possible unintended result—before long the man may be rubbing his shoulder with liniment and the little girl's dress may be headed for the dry cleaner's or washing machine.

EXERCISE 16

Devise your own picture of someone throwing a ball. Remember to color with adjectives, nouns, and adverbs as well as your verb.

Here, as our literary example, has got to be one of the all-time great action sequences, the chase scene in Chaucer's "Nun's Priest's Tale." The setting is a barnyard belonging to a certain widow and her two daughters. The cock has just been tricked by the fox and carried off on his back, and the hens, the cock's wives, have sent up a cry of alarm. The cry is taken up by the three women, and then the fun begins:

The sely widwe and eek hir doughtres two	*innocent*
Herden thise hennes crye and maken wo,	
And out at dores sterten they anoon,	*leaped*
And sien the fox toward the grove goon,	*saw*
And bar upon his bak the cok away,	
And criden, "Out, harrow, and wailaway,	*help*
Ha, ha, the fox," and after him they ran,	
And eek with staves many another man;	
Ran Colle oure dogge, and Talbot and Gerland,	

And Malkin with a distaf in hir hand,
Ran cow and calf, and eek the verray hogges,
Sore aferd for berking of the dogges   *frightened*
And shouting of the men and wommen eke.
They ronne so hem thoughte hir herte breke;   *ran*
They yelleden as feendes doon in helle;
The dokes criden as men wolde hem quelle;   *ducks/kill*
The gees for fere flowen over the trees;   *flew*
Out of the hive cam the swarm of bees;
So hidous was the noise, a, benedicite,   *bless me*
Certes, he Jakke Straw and him meinee   *company*
Ne made nevere shoutes half so shrille
Whan that they wolden any Fleming kille,
As thilke day was maad upon the fox:
Of bras they broughten bemes and of box,   *trumpets/boxwood*
Of horn, of boon, in whiche they blewe and pouped,   *bone*
And therwithal they skriked and they houped—   *shrieked/whooped*
It seemed as that hevene sholde falle.

Notice how economical Chaucer was at first in his use of verbs. Not only did the women run, so too did "many another man," the three dogs, Malkin the servant with a stick in her hand, and even the cow, calf, and hogs. There was a method to his madness; he used "run" exclusively there, so that he could surprise and charm with the added touches of the geese, also frightened, flying over the trees and the swarm of bees coming out of the hive. Sound-making reinforces all this movement—besides crying, everyone is either barking, shouting, yelling, or blowing and pooping on a variety of horns. And allusions inserted at key places add the finishing touch to the picture—the hogs ran as if their hearts would break and yelled like fiends in hell; the clamor surpassed that of Jack Straw and his men when killing Flemish folk; and finally with the added noise of the brass, boxwood, and bone horns on top of the various outcries, it sounded as if heaven would fall.

EXERCISE 17

Take your action of the previous exercise and elaborate on it so as to turn it into a whole scene. If you can't do that or don't care to, start afresh by thinking of a profession—let's say, teaching. Make a list of verbs connected with it—in this case, "talking," "lecturing," "correcting," "grading," "nagging," "sighing" etc. Follow this by writing a brief description of an individual who would perform those actions, and then put it all together.

There are almost an infinite number of other skills and tools that an aspiring poet should at least be somewhat familiar with. Below are given the highlights of the more important ones. For further information, see Edward P. J. Corbett's *Classical Rhetoric* or a good (meaning descriptive) handbook of literary terms, such as that by Holman and Harmon.

Ways of looking at things

Contemporary psychologists would surely frown on someone nowadays using personification (or prosopoeia)—investing something inanimate with human qualities—and if those human qualities turn out to be exclusively masculine, feminists are not too friendly to the idea either. But giving a human personality to something is so natural a thing for us all to engage in and has such a long, distinguished history in literature that I couldn't help but include it. Who knows, it might be making a comeback one of these days. In this example, from Thomas Gray's "Elegy in a Country Churchyard," Ambition and Grandeur have the abilities respectively of mocking and hearing:

Let not Ambition mock their useful toil,
   Their homely joys, and destiny obscure;
Nor Grandeur hear with a disdainful smile
   The short and simple annals of the poor.

Admittedly this is rather tame stuff. But take note of this passage from Wordsworth's *The Prelude*, where a specialized form of personification known as pathetic fallacy is employed—where one humanizes the great outdoors or some part of it. The poet has just recounted how he stole a boat as a boy:

   . . . lustily
I dipped my oars into the silent lake,
And, as I rose upon the stroke, my boat
Went heaving through the water like a swan;
When, from behind that craggy steep till then
The horizon's bound, a huge peak, black and huge,
As if with voluntary power instinct
Upreared its head. I struck and struck again,
And growing still in stature the grim shape
Towered up between me and the stars, and still,

For so it seemed, with purpose of its own
And measured motion like a living thing,
Strode after me. With trembling oars I turned,
And through the silent water stole my way
Back to the covert of the willow tree;
There in her mooring-place I left my bark,—
And through the meadows homeward went, in grave
And serious mood; but after I had seen
That spectacle, for many days, my brain
Worked with a dim and undetermined sense
Of unknown modes of being; o'er my thoughts
There hung a darkness, call it solitude
Or blank desertion.

EXERCISE 18

For all their usefulness, labor-saving devices like vacuum cleaners
and computers seem to be forever playing tricks on people, and you are
surely no exception. In fact, chances are you've already endowed that
misbehaving mechanical thing that seems to have a mind of its own with
a personality, maybe even a name. But just in case you haven't, do so
now, and briefly describe how it has wronged you. Sometimes this
works best in the form of a letter of complaint to the manufacturer.

But of course if you feel that you can handle personification seriously,
all fine and good. Choose an appropriate subject—and write on!

Poets of the past have also been known to address, or apostrophize,
some absent being, and sometimes, as in this selection from Wordsworth's "Tintern Abbey," it was a personification of a natural force.
After expatiating on the curative powers of Nature, which includes the
river Wye, Wordsworth went on to say:

If this
Be but a vain belief, yet, oh! how oft—
In darkness and amid the many shapes
Of joyless daylight; when the fretful stir
Unprofitable, and the fever of the world,
Have hung upon the beatings of my heart—
How oft, in spirit, have I turned to thee,
O sylvan Wye! thou wanderer thro' the woods,
How often has my spirit turned to thee!

One of my teachers in graduate school once said that the sounds in
the phrase "O sylvan Wye" were among the most beautiful in our
language. Pronounce it, isn't it so? Say it out loud—O sylvan Wye!

EXERCISE 19

Refer to the last exercise and write an apostrophe or address to your personification—that, or a new letter of complaint to your contraption itself.

Substituting synonyms

If, at a certain point in your writing, you don't want to repeat yourself and would rather not use a pronoun, there are any number of ways to handle the situation with style. You can refer to a part of that something (synecdoche)—for example, "guns" for "weapons," "meat," for "entree," "hands" for "employees," "silver" for "change." You can substitute some attributive or suggestive word (metonymy)—like "the homeless" for people who are destitute. You can use a descriptive word or phrase instead (periphrasis)—"slave driver" for "employer"—or a proper name for a quality associated with your subject—"Sleeping Beauty" for some sleepy-head.

EXERCISE 20

Just for practice, go back over some list of yours—a grocery list works splendidly here—and write in substitutes in one fashion or another.

Irreverent references

It has been said that good liars make good writers (and vice versa), so, while telling untruths is of dubious value in real life, it sometimes pays off on paper. Two modes of truth-distortion are exaggeration (hyperbole)—as in, "the face that launched a thousand ships"—and understatement (litotes)—"crime of passion" for "brutal murder."

EXERCISE 21

Using your grocery list as a basis, write a short account of going shopping to purchase the items on it, employing hyperbole throughout. Then take the same account and revise it, understating everything that you've overstated.

Asking a rhetorical question (erotema), that is, phrasing something in the form of a question for effect, and not to seek an answer, is yet another way of saying something without stating it—"Who's afraid of the big bad wolf?"

And finally, there is irony, the conveying of a meaning opposite of that intended. An excellent example of the use of irony can be found

in Shakespeare's *Julius Caesar*, when Antony, empowered by Brutus
and Caesar's other assassins to give a funeral oration for Caesar, refers
again and again to Brutus as an honorable man. We shall have occasion
to examine Antony's Funeral Oration in more detail in the next chapter in connection with refrains, but you may want to look at it now.

EXERCISE 22

Who has never waxed ironical? Write an ironical comment on this
book so far or another you've read recently. Stick in a rhetorical question if you can.

Purposeful omissions

At times, instead of substituting one expression for another or being
oblique, you may want to omit a not-too-necessary word or two from a
passage deliberately (ellipsis) for emphasis. For example, you could
write "When in doubt, leave out" for "When you are in doubt, leave
it out." This form of omission should be used sparingly lest your writing
lapse into telegrams.

EXERCISE 23

Take your ironical comment and make it more emphatic by striking
out some words.

In the same fashion, where it seems appropriate for the sake of sense
or sound or both, you may want to leave out conjunctions between a
series of related clauses (asyndeton)—as in Caesar's famous statement
with respect to Gaul, "I came, I saw, I conquered."

EXERCISE 24

Find the piece of action writing that you worked up in Exercise 17 and
create new effects by getting rid of some of the conjunctions.

Word play and playing with words

Remember our puns in Chapter One? The ones with the names like
diseases? Why not turn back to page 8 and review them now. In fact—

EXERCISE 25

Why not try your hand at some fresh puns. One of each kind, if you
please!

And while you're at it in Chapter One, why not take another look at what Lewis Carroll's Humpty Dumpty had to say about portmanteau words on page 5 and review your own portmanteaus in Exercise 7, then—

EXERCISE 26

Dream up some new portmanteaus. Let's say three. But of course if you have some good ones, repeat them. And if you like someone else's, appropriate.

Did you ever hear of an oxymoron? No, it has nothing to do with cattle or retardation. It's the name of another way of messing about with words; it's the use of two terms, usually an adjective and noun, that are contradictory—for example, "sweet pain" and "cheerful pessimist." It would be hard to beat Blake's "Marriage hearse"—but try.

EXERCISE 27

Come up with a few oxymorons of your own. And if you don't know where to start, go back to your description of a person looking at his or her watch in Exercise 13 and insert some there.

Yet another way of playing with words is to transpose the initial letters of two that normally belong together (spoonerism)—"blushing crow" for "crushing blow," that sort of thing.

EXERCISE 28

Make up a spoonerism, but bear in mind that to be really effective, yours ought to have some meaning, and it should be absurdly tangential to your original phrase.

Finally, there is antihimera or, simply, using one part of speech for another, as in "The rejected suitor dogged her footsteps" (noun "dog" as verb), "the catch of the day" (verb "catch" as noun), "She is a very-soon type of person" (adverbs "very soon" as adjective), and "Chew it up good" (adjective "good" as adverb). If you decide to become an advertising copy writer instead of a poet, being skillful in the use of antihimera will come in very handy. According to one school of thought, "Winston tastes good *like* a cigarette should" meant the ruin of modern English grammar.

EXERCISE 29

Do what you will with antihimera. One can very well turn this into a can-you-top-this sort of game.

QUAINT CURIOSITIES

Besides playing with the words themselves, you can also play with their spelling. You can add syllables to the front (prosthesis), middle (epenthesis), or end (proparalepsis)—"besmirched" for "smirched," "orientating" for "orienting," "embrasure" for "embrace." You can subtract in the same way (aphaereis, syncope, apocope)—"'kay" for "okay," "o'er" for "over," and "shrink" for "head shrinker."

Also, you can transpose letters of words (metathesis)—"traispe" for "traipse." And indeed at times in our language this is and has been done unintentionally, as with "ask," which was "axe" before 1066 A.D. and through usage is on the road of returning to "axe" now.

Leave it to the Greeks—they did everything with words and had names for it. You can change the very sounds of words (antisthecon)—make "dreary" into "Duh-reary" and "hermaphrodite" into "morphy-dye."

EXERCISE 30

Have a ball.

A final word is in order respecting all that has passed here in this chapter. Get into the habit of using these tools and aids, and using them effectively both as to sense and sound. But if you cannot do that, don't force things—leave out. Above all, unless you are doing so deliberately, don't overuse any of the above, or you risk being accused of setting technique before text—of showing off verbal ability at the expense of meaning and depth.

CHAPTER FOUR

Traditional English verse and how it works: rhythm and meter

Most poets nowadays write in free verse, which as you are no doubt aware, is not governed by any external rules or, as we say in literary circles, has no standard rhythm or meter and is without any rhyme to speak of. And certainly unless you are of an antiquarian bent, you should strive to be a part of your time and write in free verse—but where this book is concerned, not so fast! English and American poets have been exploring their ideas in unshackled verse only for the last hundred years or so; before that it was all rules and regulations, and indeed, free verse became increasingly popular in the last century as a reaction to those strictures. My feeling is that a better understanding of where those poets were coming from and what one's own destination is can be obtained by re-living the past. So hold off on writing free verse for a while and in this chapter and the three following come with me into the egg—the egg of traditional English verse—and then out again.

A question arises: When did traditional English verse begin? The answer would seem to be with the beginning of the English language, that is, when the Angles and Saxons first broke away from their Germanic brethren on the Continent in the fifth century and settled in what is now Great Britain—but this is not so. In 1066 the language that they spoke, which we today call Anglo-Saxon or Old English, became subject to an unlooked-for influence. The Normans invaded their country, and for some two centuries the official language—that spoken by the upper classes—was French. Thus by the time the two populations became one and English re-asserted itself, it had lost much of its Germanic flavor and was full of French loan words. The same thing happened in poetry; the native English form gave way to French and Latin ones brought by the Normans, and then there was a blending—and out of that blending, beginning gradually in the latter part of the fourteenth century, emerged what we like to think of as traditional English verse.

Let's take a moment to look back at our poetical roots—our real poetical roots—and sneak up on our subject of traditional English verse. Anglo-Saxon or Old English verse consisted of lines marked by a pause (or caesura) in the middle. Each half-line (before and after the pause) contained two accented or heavily stressed syllables and a variable number of unaccented or lightly stressed syllables. The initial letters of three of the accented syllables were the same (or alliterated). Here is a nonsense line in modern English by way of illustration:

Tátter for Tómmy   túnnel in hánd

EXERCISE 1

It is important to understand what this original (or pre-traditional) form of English verse was like, so repeat the line aloud several times, emphasizing the accents and alliterated "t"'s more than one normally would, and pausing significantly in mid-line.

Now here's a hymn by a seventh century monk named Caedmon, with the spelling modified for ease of reading. Even so, if you're at all gun-shy about foreign languages, don't faint.

Nu we shulon hérian   Heófon-riches Weard,
(Now we shall praise   Heaven-kingdom's guardian,)
Méotodes méachte   and His mód-gethanc,
(God's power   and His understanding,)
wéorc Wúldor-Faeder,   swa He wúndra gehwaes,
(work of the Glory-Father   as He of each wonder,)
oéche Drychten,   ór ónstealde.
(the eternal Lord   the foundation laid.)
He áerest shop   eórthan bearnum
(He first created   for men's children
Héofon to hrófe,   hálig Shieppend;
(Heaven for a roof   holy Creator;)
tha míddan-geard   mánn-cynnes Weard,
(the middle earth   mankind's guardian,)
oéche Drychten   aéfter teode
(the eternal Lord   after made)
fírum fóldan   Fréa eall-michtig.
(for men, the earth   Ruler almighty.)

Note that the whole work is written in a block like a paragraph and at the same time that each of its lines is a thing unto itself, a unit—but a loose unit because of the different number of unaccented or lightly stressed syllables on each. Monotony is further alleviated from line to line through varied numbers of accented or heavily stressed syllables and alliterations, though not all that much.

EXERCISE 2

To get into the swing of things further, may I suggest that you listen to a recording of Caedmon's hymn made by the distinguished scholar J.B. Bessinger, then repeat it or a part of it aloud, getting your body into the act as with our other repeating exercises.

Verse of this kind continued to be written in the hinterlands of England long after the arrival of the Normans, but in and around London, English poets came under the influence of French and Latin verse, which was written in stanzas with a set number of lines and sound correspondences at the ends, or end-rhymes. The French favored lines ten syllables long, and Latin verse had the added feature of a regular pattern of alternating accented or heavily stressed and unaccented or lightly stressed syllables. One example will suffice to make the difference between them and Anglo-Saxon verse clear; this is the first stanza of a playful Goliardic or student song parodying the sacrament of Confession:

Estuans intrinsecus
ira vehe*menti*
In amaritudine
loquor meae *menti*

(I seethe within in mighty wrath, in bitterness I thus address my spirit.)

EXERCISE 3

Doing is knowing. For the sake of truly feeling the difference between Anglo-Saxon verse and the new-fangled French and Latin forms of the eleventh century, repeat these four lines aloud as well, emphasizing the heavily accented syllables (marked with a ´) and the rhymes:

És-tu-ańs in-triń-se-cús
i´-ra vé-he-mén-Tĺ!
Iń a-már-i-tú-di-ńe
ló-quor mé-ae mén-Tĺ!

By Chaucer's time (ca. 1343–1400), the English language, now known as Middle English, was pretty well Frenchified, and a new English poetry had come into being, characterized by lines written either in stanza form or in paragraphs and consisting of ten alternating lightly and heavily accented syllables and end-rhymes. Here, as an example, is the celebrated opening to Chaucer's masterpiece, *The Canterbury Tales*.

Notice the words of obvious French origin, like "vertu," "engendred," "tendre," and "corages," as well as the hang-overs from native English, like "droghte" and "swich":

Whan that Aprill with his shoures soote	*its/sweet*
The droghte of March hath perced to the roote,	
And bathed every veyne in swich licour	*such/liquid*
Of which vertu engendred is the flour;	
Whan Zephirus eek with his sweete breeth	*also*
Inspired hath in every holt and heeth	*grove/field*
The tendre croppes, and the yonge sonne	*shoots*
Hath in the Ram his halve cours yronne,	
And smale foweles maken melodye,	
That slepen al the nyght with open ye	*eye*
(So priketh hem nature in hir corages);	*them*
Thanne longen folk to goon on pilgrimages,	*go*
And palmeres for to seken straunge strondes,	
To ferne halwes, kowthe in sondry londes;	*known*
And specially from every shires ende	
Of Engelond to Caunterbury they wende,	
The hooly blisful martir for to seke,	
That hem hath holpen whan that they were seeke.	*helped/sick*

EXERCISE 4

Bessinger made a recording of selections, including the Prologue, from *The Canterbury Tales* as well. This should be played, or one should listen to some other expert in Middle English pronunciation reading the above aloud—and then one should imitate.

Within another two hundred years, the English language had come into its own—as of then we designate it as Modern English, though it sounds "old" to most lay people—and English verse written in stanzas or paragraphs, with lines of alternating lightly and heavily stressed syllables, unrhymed as well as rhymed, was established as the norm. This opening stanza to Christopher (Kit) Marlowe's "The Passionate Shepherd to His Love" (1599) says it all:

Come live with me and be my love,
And we will all the pleasures prove
That valleys, groves, hills, and fields,
Woods, or steepy mountain yields.

EXERCISE 5

To round out our little history, repeat these lines of Marlowe's aloud too; just keep in mind that the pronunciation would have been a little different from our own today—as different as Oxford English is from middle American. Note: the heavily stressed syllables are indicated by ´, the lightly by ˘.

Come live with me and be my love,
And we will all the pleasures prove
That valleys, groves, hills, and fields,
Woods, or steepy mountain yields.

Sometimes it helps to review by repeating all of the poems above, one after the other.

The principal features of traditional English verse, then, are the beat, or rhythm that results from a uniform alternation of weak and strong syllables, and how long that rhythm is per line, or meter, plus sound correspondences, or rhyme, usually coming at the ends of lines. Now it's time to home in on these matters—first the beat.

THERE ARE SYLLABLES AND SYLLABLES

But before we can do this, it is necessary to make sure that we all know what a syllable is and can recognize one at will. Ah come on, everyone knows that, some of you are saying. Well, maybe yes, maybe no, let's see. But before you grow impatient, let me add that we'll be cutting our teeth on *haiku* at the same time. You don't know what *haiku* is? Well, you'll find out in a few moments—just bear in mind for now that it's not something to eat.

All words consist of one or more syllables. A syllable is produced by a single impulse of the speaking apparatus and thus can be a vowel or diphthong by itself (for example, the "o" in "oval" or "ai" in "eyebrow") or a vowel or diphthong flanked on either or both sides by one or more consonants (the "bo" in "limbo," "bor" in "labor," "bort" in "abort").

When a consonant comes between two vowels, there are two systems of breakdown, an American and an English. According to the American, the consonant is a part of the first syllable, according to the English it's a part of the second—as in this example:

American: ven-om
English: ve-nom

We shall be using the English system, which may take a bit of getting used to.

EXERCISE 6

Separate the following words into syllables and count them: "balance," "garbage," "fabricate," "articulate," "co-operation," "mispronunciation," and "individuality." Be sure to use the English system when it comes to the "l" in "balance" and so on.

When you're done, compare your answers with your classmates' if you're taking a course; if you're alone or there is disagreement, check it out by consulting the *Oxford English Dictionary* (*OED*) or some other dictionary based on the English system. Counting the syllables in the words above is a very important first step, so if you had too many wrong, or experienced difficulty with this exercise, turn to the beginning of the chapter (or where you will) and practice counting some more—until you feel comfortable doing it.

Then, and only then, go on to—

EXERCISE 7

Count up the syllables in the following excerpts from poems, and record the total on each line as well as in each word:

a.
When I have fears that I may cease to be
   Before my pen has glean'd my teeming brain,
Before high-piléd books, in charact'ry,
   Hold like rich garners the full-ripen'd grain

b.
A *little learning* is a dang'rous thing;
Drink deep, or taste not the Pierian spring.
There shallow draughts intoxicate the brain,
And drinking largely sobers us again.

c.
I was thy neighbour once, thou rugged Pile!
Four summer weeks I dwelt in sight of thee:
I saw thee every day; and all the while
Thy Form was sleeping on a glassy sea.

d.
The king sits in Dumferling town,
Drinking the blude-reid wine;
"O whar will I get a guid sailor,
To sail this ship of mine?"

Here are the answers per line:

c: 1 (10), 2 (10), 3 (10), 4 (8); d: 1 (10), 2 (10), 3 (8), 4 (6).
a: 1 (10), 2 (10), 3 (10), 4 (10); b: 1 (10), 2 (10), 3 (10), 4 (10);

Now for further practice at counting syllables, let's try our hand at composing some *haiku*. What is *haiku*? It's a short Japanese poem that goes back to antiquity and was revived in the seventeenth century, then later in this century was imported into English, where it has enjoyed a considerable vogue. That is, it was sort of imported because Japanese is so different from our language, among other things, their verbs coming at the ends of sentences, objects before prepositions. Thus *haiku* in English was always at best imitation—pseudo-*haiku*.

Most important, as far as we are concerned, a *haiku* is supposed to consist of seventeen syllables, no more nor less, arranged in three lines of five, seven, and five syllables respectively. Ideally the goal is to depict nature as a whole through one small aspect, and somewhere on those lines there should be a *kigo* or "season word" hinting at the time of year appropriate to the context—some symbol like our harvest moon for autumn, for instance—while the last word ought to be a noun or an emotional ejaculation, something like our "Oh" or "Ah." Other features of *haiku*, like *renso*, a throwing together of unrelated images, and a simulation of *satori* or Zen enlightenment through a sudden leap from the second to the third line, tend to get lost in translation.

Here is an example from one of the masters:

Shaking his loose skin,
A tired old horse scares away
A white butterfly
            —Issa Kobayashi (1763–1827)

EXERCISE 8

Try your hand at one or more *haiku*. Above all, be sure to have the proper number of syllables on each line—remember, five-seven-five. After all, that's the major point of this exercise.

When you are finished, have someone verify that your lines indeed consist of five, seven, and five syllables, and of course, if there's occasion, you should read your creation or best creation aloud. If it turns out that you haven't abided by the rule of five-seven-five, keep working at it until you do.

But that is not the end of our concern with syllables—indeed, it is just the beginning. In English, words of two syllables or more are pronounced with more emphasis on one syllable than the other or others, or are accented as we are accustomed to saying. For instance, the "re" in "recent" is so emphasized; if we put the accent on the last syllable, it would be "resent." Being able to find accented syllables is our next task. But because of the polyglot origin of English words, there is no set rule as to accentuation, and so to do that, one can only pronounce and re-pronounce—or else look in the dictionary, which for us is self-defeating.

EXERCISE 9

Let's begin simply with two-syllable words: a) garbage, b) decay, c) lazy, d) decade, e) because, f) murder. Divide each one into syllables first, and then decide on the accented one. Use a ´ to indicate accents.

Here are the answers:

a) first, b) second, c) first, d) first, e) second, f) first.

If you experienced difficulty with this exercise, don't go on. Look for more two-syllable words in this chapter—or anywhere!—and practice.

EXERCISE 10

Now let's find accented syllables in some three- and four-syllable words: a) hideous, b) insanity, c) bothersome, d) ridiculous, e) photograph, f) statistic, g) photographer. Remember to divide the word up into syllables first if you haven't already done that.

Check your answers:

a) first, b) second, c) first, d) second, e) first, f) second, g) second.

By now you should be an old hand at this, so—

EXERCISE 11

Try finding the accents in the following phrases: a) Supreme Being, b) Happy Birthday, c) aware again, d) breakfast cereal. Take your time with these even if you've had a perfect score up to this point.

See how you did:

a) second, first; b) first, first; c) second, second; d) first, first.

Now for the pièce de résistance—

EXERCISE 12

Find the accented syllables in the polysyllabic words in the stanzas in Exercise 7 above. Caution: make sure that the words are all correctly divided into syllables before you begin.

If there is some disagreement among members of the class or you're using this book by yourself, consult the *OED* or some reasonable equivalent this time.

We are now ready to tackle the rhythm and meter of traditional English verse.

ENGLISH VERSE HAS FEET

As we have seen in the example of Marlowe's "The Passionate Shepherd to His Love," traditional English verse consists of lines of alternating lightly stressed and heavily stressed syllables. A single unit of such syllables is called a foot, and the prevailing foot in a given work identifies the rhythm for us.

In the first line of Marlowe's poem, for instance, the feet (separated by slashes) are all made up of a single lightly stressed followed by a heavily stressed syllable:

Come live/ with me/ and be/ my love.

So too are the majority of feet in the rest of the stanza (and indeed in the balance of the poem). Such a foot, consisting of a lightly stressed followed by a heavily stressed syllable, is called an *iamb*, and thus the rhythm of "The Passionate Shepherd to His Love" is said to be *iambic*.

The Greeks had countless numbers of feet, but in English, only three others have been used:

anapest—two lightly stressed syllables plus a heavily stressed one (˘ ˘ ´). Think: cha-cha-CHA.

trochee—one heavily stressed syllable plus a lightly stressed syllable, the opposite of the *iamb* in other words (´ ˘). "Recent" and "bedlam" are good examples of single word trochees.

dactyl—one heavily stressed followed by two lightly stressed syllables (´ ˘ ˘). Think of a waltz: UM-pa-pa.

But the fact of the matter is that most English verse is iambic. While no one to my knowledge has ever done a count, I'm willing to wager that there is more poetry, far more, written in iambs than the sum total in all other feet. So we shall be dealing here in the main with iambs and iambic verse, and touch on the others only in passing. Later on in Chapter Seven there will be some notable examples of poems written in anapests and trochees.

EXERCISE 13

The following are isolated lines from some of the snippets of verse that we worked with in Exercise 7; they are all iambic. Analyze them—or as we say, scan them—marking off weak and strong stresses and separating the feet with slashes. It's a good idea to divide polysyllabic words up into separate syllables first, and this you've already done; simply refer back to Exercise 7, find the lines, and copy:

a. Before my pen has glean'd my teeming brain
b. And drinking largely sobers us again
c. I saw thee every day; and all the while

How did you make out? Well, I hope—and trust:

c. I saw/ thee ev-/ (e)ry day;/ and all/ the while
b. And drin-/ king large-/ ly so-/ bers us/ a-gain
a. Be-fore/ my pen/ has glean'd/ my teem-/ ing brain

But if you didn't, you might want to practice with these lines a little, saying them over in a kind of chant, while giving extra emphasis to the heavy stresses and less emphasis to the light ones. Sometimes it helps to beat out the heavy ones by tapping your foot or slapping your thigh with your hand, or even banging a ruler on the edge of the desk.

EXERCISE 14

Create three of your own lines of iambs, using those above as models. When you have them, scan in the same way.

You should not have come to grief with this, and assuming that you didn't—

EXERCISE 15

Create some lines of iambs without reference to your models, and scan them as well.

As to the other rhythms, anapests (�‿ �‿ ´) and trochees (´ �‿) have been used by poets on occasion to good effect, but works written exclusively in dactyls (´ �‿ ˘) are rare because it is very difficult to sustain an Um-pa-pa measure in English beyond a few lines. Even so—

EXERCISE 16

Identify the following words or phrases as an anapest, trochee, or dactyl: a) birdhouse, b) in-between, c) ramshackle, d) as a rule, e) in a fix.

a) trochee, b) dactyl, c) trochee, d) anapest, e) anapest.

How close did you come? If not too close, persevere—tap or clap it out—but don't lose any sleep over it:

EXERCISE 17

Scan the following snippets and identify, remembering to divide the polysyllabic words into separate syllables first:

a. Piping down the valleys wild
b. When the voices of children are heard on the green
c. After the pangs of a desperate lover

As I have indicated, these rhythms have not been used too often in English, especially the dactylic. Note, if you haven't, the extra syllable in item a and the odd fourth foot in c:

a. Pi-ping/ dówn thĕ/ val-léys/ wíld
b. When thĕ/ voi-/ cés of/ chil-/ dren áre/ heard on/ the gréen
c. Af-tĕr thĕ/ pángs of thĕ/ des-pĕr-átĕ/ ló-ver

So much, for the moment at least, respecting rhythm. Now let's move on to the other matter at hand, meter. Much easier to grasp than rhythm, a meter of a given poem is purely and simply the number of feet usually found in the lines, and is indicated with the Greek words for the numbers: monometer (one), dimeter (two), trimeter (three), tetrameter (four), pentameter (five), hexameter (six), and so on. For instance, the meter of Christopher Marlowe's poem is tetrameter—

Come líve/ wĭth mé/ ănd bé/ mў lóve = 4 feet
Ănd wé/ shăll áll/ thĕ pléa-/ sŭres próve = 4 feet

and we would therefore designate it rhythmically and metrically as iambic tetrameter.

EXERCISE 19

Go back to the lines in Exercise 17, count up the number of feet, and give each a rhythmo-metrical designation, as I did "The Passionate Shepherd."

Here we are:

a) trochaic tetrameter, b) anapestic tetrameter, c) dactylic tetrameter.

EXERCISE 20

Now go back to the lines in Exercise 13 and do the same.

Surprise:

all three are iambic pentameter.

On the other hand, it should not be a surprise at all—for just as most traditional English verse has been written in iambs, a good deal of that iambic verse—as much as 75% I've heard—is in pentameter. This includes most of *The Canterbury Tales*, the better part of Shakespeare's plays, and Milton's major works, including *Paradise Lost*.

Iambic pentameter occurs in both rhymed and unrhymed states; when in the latter, it is known as blank verse. Later on in Chapter Six we will be looking at examples of both types and trying our hands at each. For the moment we must address ourselves in general terms to rhyme, the other major feature of traditional English verse.

When I am giving a course involving this material, it is at this point that students become impatient and want to rush ahead, and end up composing something of their own in one of the rhythms and meters covered above. By all means do so too, if you feel that you must. But if you do, I suggest that you confine your efforts to iambs, preferably to iambic pentameter, and bear in mind that the lines we analyzed above in Exercise 20 represent exceptions to the rule rather than the rule in their regularity—that is, in their consisting of five perfect iambs, no more nor less. To anticipate one of the main concerns in Chapter Six, it's variations of that regular line that make iambic pentameter (as well as other forms of iambic verse) effective.

EXERCISE 21

See for yourself; scan the first three lines of the stanza from which one of our examples was taken:

A *little learning* is a dang'rous thing;
Drink deep, or taste not the Pierian spring.
There shallow draughts intoxicate the brain,
Ănd drĭn-/ kĭng lárge-/ lў só-/ bĕrs ús/ ă-gáin.

With this clearly understood, do write something. But before you do, you may want to practice up a little more at scansion.

EXERCISE 22

Here are two juicy morsels to work on. Remember to break the poly-syllabic words up into separate syllables first:

SHE DWELT AMONG THE UNTRODDEN WAYS
by William Wordsworth

She dwelt among the untrodden ways
  Beside the springs of Dove,
A Maid whom there were none to praise
  And very few to love:

A violet by a mossy stone
  Half hidden from the eye!
—Fair as a star, when only one
  Is shining in the sky.

She lived unknown, and few could know
  When Lucy ceased to be;
But she is in her grave, and, oh,
  The difference to me!

OZYMANDIAS
by Percy Bysshe Shelley

I met a traveller from an antique land
Who said: Two vast and trunkless legs of stone
Stand in the desert . . . Near them, on the sand,
Half sunk, a shattered visage lies, whose frown,
And wrinkled lip, and sneer of cold command,

Tell that its sculptor well those passions read
Which yet survive, stamped on these lifeless things,
The hand that mocked them, and the heart that fed:
And on the pedestal these words appear:
"My name is Ozymandias, king of kings:
Look on my works, ye Mighty, and despair!"
Nothing beside remains. Round the decay
Of that colossal wreck, boundless and bare
The lone and level sands stretch far away.

If these two tasks prove mind-boggling, as well they might, not to worry. Simply push on to the next chapter and try again after you've gone through the first section of Chapter Six.

CHAPTER FIVE

Rhyming and other echoes

Rhyme can be defined as a repetition of like sounds, and was an important ingredient of traditional English verse from Chaucer on. Usually, though by no means always, occurring at the ends of lines, rhyming in the hands of a dullard is boring and silly, but as practiced by a master it can be superb, adding that finishing touch to the meaning of a poem. The poet offers a sound and an echo of it, and before the echo dies out, offers another sound and echo and another, and so on, or perhaps plays with a few sounds, going back and forth from one to the other. You get the picture—the poem just rings with sound.

SIMPLE RHYMING

"Uppon a Deedmans Hed" by fifteenth-century poet John Skelton is as good a place as any to begin. Skelton was just mad for rhyme and his every-which-way use of it is somehow strangely modern:

Youre ugly tokyn
My mynd hath brokyn
From worldly lust;
For I have dyscust
We ar but dust,
And dy we must.
  It is generall
To be mortall:
I have well espyde
No man may hym hyde
From deth holow-eyed,
With synnews wyderyd,   *withered*
With bonys shyderyd,   *shattered*
With hys worme-etyn maw
And hys gastly jaw
Gaspyng asyde,
Nakyd of hyde,
Neyther flesh nor fell.   *skin*
  Then, by my councell,
Loke that ye spell   *study*
Well thys gospell:

For wherso we dwell,
Deth wyll us quell
And with us mell.   *mix*
    For all oure pamperde paunchys,
There may no fraunchys   *franchise*
Nor worldly blys
Redeme us from this:
Oure days be datyd
To be checkmatyd,
With drawttys of deth   *drafts*
Stoppyng oure breth;
Oure eyen synkyng,
Oure bodys stynkyng,
Oure gummys grynnyng,
Oure soulys brynnyng!   *burning*
To whom then shall we sew
For to have rescew,
But to swete Jesu
On us then for to rew?
    O goodly chyld
Of Mary mylde,
Then be oure shylde!
That we be not exylyd
To the dyne dale   *dun*
Of boteles bale,   *bootless/sorrow*
Nor to the lake
Of fendys blake.   *fiends/black*
    But graunt us grace
To se thy face,
And to purchace
Thyne hevenly place
And thy palace,
Full of solace,
Above the sky,
That is so hy,
Eternally
To beholde and se
The Trynyte!
    Amen.

EXERCISE 1

Write a brief response to this piece of Skelton's, paying him back in his own metrical and rhyming coin. Rhyming is always great fun—it can be like gorging yourself on ice cream when you were a kid. Sometimes it pays off to go partners on this first exercise in rhyming or work in a small group. And if you're alone, this may be a good time to get hold of a friend, even one not too interested in poetry. Who knows, you might make a convert.

Rhymes can be either complete, meaning with an exact correspondence between one or more final vowels (after Skelton's example, "sky"/"high") or vowel-consonant combinations ("death"/"breath"), or partial ("bale"/"grace"). Complete rhymes involving words of a single syllable are obviously the most elemental and direct, and can produce a striking effect. Consider, for instance, Wordsworth's "A Slumber Did My Spirit Seal." Note how the "r" sound of "rolled round" is reinforced by those in "fears"/"years" and "force"/"course," and the related "l" sound in "seal"/"feel."

A slumber did my spirit seal;
  I had no human fears:
She seemed a thing that could not feel
  The touch of earthly years.

No motion has she now, no force;
  She neither hears nor sees;
Rolled round in earth's diurnal course,
  With rocks, and stones, and trees.

"Sees"/ "trees" extends the rhymes of the first stanza and thus adds to the rolling round (as does the repetition of "and" in the final line). According to some scholars, by the way, the "she" is the "I" 's spirit (the anima or soul being feminine in Latin), and the subject of the poem is a profound personal experience.

EXERCISE 2

I'm a great believer in imitating, as you know—a poet-in-the-making can learn much from it I feel; to me it is akin to a novice painter making copies from the masters in a museum. Try an imitation of this cross-rhymed poem of alternating iambic tetrameter and trimeter lines, choosing a serious or even somber subject this time. But if you don't feel up to it, do the rhymes with nonsense lines at least.

Besides pairs of monosyllabic words, it is possible to rhyme one of them with the initial or final syllable of a two-syllable word ("he"/ "plenty"; "rain"/ "stainless"), and one or the other parts of two-syllable words ("crafty"/ "drafted"; "dissent"/ "prevent").

EXERCISE 3

If you are still chewing on the poem that you did for the previous exercise and feel perhaps that the rhymes were forced, work on it some more and include two-syllable words if necessary.

Rhymes involving two or more syllables ("recent"/"decent"; "garage"/"barrage") are, of course, possible, but have always been considered the province of light verse; for instance, critics took Wordsworth severely to task in his own time for rhyming "shocked her" with "doctor" in his supposedly serious poem "The Idiot Boy." His younger contemporary Lord Byron made a profession out of irreverence, as is here demonstrated in these stanzas from his magnificent satiric epic, *Don Juan* (pronounced "jéw-an"). Notice in the first instance how Byron managed to eke out "new one"/ "true one," and then went on to top it off with "Juan," and in the second instance how he had absolutely the last word with "intellectual" and "hen-pecked you all":

I want a hero: an uncommon want,
   When every year and month sends forth a new one,
Till, after cloying the gazettes with cant,
   The age discovers he is not the true one;
Of such as these I should not care to vaunt,
   I'll therefore take our ancient friend Don Juan—
We all have seen him, in the pantomime,
Sent to the Devil somewhat ere his time. . . .

'T is pity learnéd virgins ever wed
   With persons of no sort of education,
Or gentlemen, who, though well born and bred,
   Grow tired of scientific conversation:
I don't choose to say much upon this head,
   I'm a plain man, and in a single station,
But—Oh! ye lords of ladies intellectual,
Inform us truly, have they not hen-pecked you all?

What makes the last two rhymes particularly effective is Byron's restraint until then in the stanza with respect to clever sound correspondences.

EXERCISE 4

Here's a chance to do your stuff as a wit, using rhymes of two syllables or more. You have a choice—add to or revise your response to

Skelton in Exercise 1, or work up something new. We'll be covering ⌐ particular stanza form—known as *ottava rima*—later in Chapter Seven, but if it appeals to you, by all means take a stab at an imitation now.

Partial rhymes of a variety of types have been (and can be) used to achieve a dissonant effect, no matter whether a poem is serious or silly. First of all, there is *near rhyme*, in which the consonants following the vowels in a given pair of syllables are related but not identical—as in "grunt" and "trundle." *Eye rhyme*, in which the rhyming syllables are spelled alike but pronounced differently, is another old standby—consider Marlowe's "Come live with me and be my *love*,/ And we will all the pleasures *prove*." *Assonance*, a correspondence of vowels alone—"neck"/ "met"—has also been around a good long while, as has *consonance*, a correspondence of consonants alone—"fox"/"annex." We have already met *alliteration*, in which the initial consonants of words are the same, in Anglo-Saxon poetry, which allowed for initial vowels as well—but in case you have forgotten, there's always "Peter Piper picked a peck of pickled peppers" to remind you. The *sine qua non* of partial rhyming is a combination of assonance and consonance where the corresponding vowels and consonants are not in the same syllable—as in "fox"/ "onyx."

The secret of using partial rhymes effectively is, as with other things, not to overuse them. No better example of discretion in this respect can be found than this ostensibly simple poem by Blake with the deceptively simple title of "Spring":

> Sound the Flute!
> Now it's mute.
> Birds delight
> Day and Night;
> Nightingale
> In the dale,
> Lark in Sky,
> Merrily,
> Merrily, Merrily, to welcome in the Year.

> Little Boy,
> Full of joy;
> Little Girl,
> Sweet and small;
> Cock does crow,
> So do you;
> Merry voice,
> Infant noise,
> Merrily, Merrily, to welcome in the Year.

> Little Lamb,
> Here I am;
> Come and lick
> My white neck;
> Let me pull
> Your soft Wool;
> Let me kiss
> Your soft face:
> Merrily, Merrily, we welcome in the Year.

In the first stanza the rhymes are all complete; however, there is a hint of things to come in the alliteration of "d"'s in "delight," "day," and "dale" and of the "n"'s in "now," "night" and "nightingale," and in the eye rhyme of "sky" and "merrily." In the second stanza Blake became more openly daring with the consonance of "girl" and "small," assonance of "voice" and "noise," and near assonance of "crow" and "you." And in the third stanza he played with consonance—"lick"/ "neck," "pull"/"Wool," and finally "kiss"/"face."

Notice further how careful he was to begin each venture into dissonance, let us call it, with a pure rhyme—"Boy"/"Joy"; "Lamb"/"am." This is the way of music, great classical music—the way of Mozart and Beethoven. The repetition of "Merrily, Merrily, to welcome in the Year" and its variant with "we" at the end of each stanza—technically known as a *refrain*—comes almost as a kind of taunt—"Look what I can do? Can you do better?"

EXERCISE 5

Here, for starters, is a list of the different kinds of partial rhymes with further examples:

near rhyme—"dress"/ "pressed."
eye rhyme—"wind" (noun)/ "kind."
assonance—"tank"/ "last."
consonance—"bad"/ "good."
alliteration—"fellow"/ "freaks."

Come up with an additional example of each and write it in your notebook.

If you're in a class, these should be read aloud. Be sure to jot down any good ones that you hear for future reference. If you're using this book by yourself, it often proves helpful to look through an anthology for other examples.

EXERCISE 6

Make use of each kind of partial rhyme to good effect in your poem responding to Skelton's. Remember that the secret of success, even when writing broad comedy, is the avoidance of excess.

In the final half of the last century conventional rhyming began to seem cloying to some poets and they took to using partial rhymes to cut down on the tinkle. In "Sailing to Byzantium," Yeats boldly did just this with the *ottava rima* stanza, which by his time had broad associations with satire because of Byron's *Don Juan*. However, as with Blake above, he exercised considerable restraint in the use of incomplete rhyming, and the result turned out to be a serious statement that in other, less skillful hands might not have worked at all. Take a look at the poem some time, and note especially how he set his own pace in the first stanza with "young"/"trees"/"song"/"seas"/"long"/"dies"/"neglect"/ "intellect."

EXERCISE 7

Get out the serious poem that you composed for Exercise 2 and worked on anew in Exercise 3, and try for dissonance in an appropriate place with one of the varieties of partial rhyme.

A final word remains to be said about rhyme placement and related matters. As was pointed out before, both full and partial rhymes were usually found at the ends of lines, marking a slight pause there for the sake of emphasis and adornment—or in more learned terms, setting off the line as a semantic and sonar entity. When two line-ends rhyme consecutively, the lines are called a *couplet*—the final pair of lines in the *ottava rima* stanza is a couplet. Where the rhymes alternate with others, it is called *cross-rhyming*—see the first six lines of the same stanza, also Wordsworth's "A Slumber Did My Spirit Seal." Occasionally an *envelope* arrangement is used—a rhyme, a couplet, followed by the first rhyme—as in the opening to Keats' "On First Looking into Chapman's Homer":

Much have I travell'd in the realms of gold,
   And many goodly states and kingdoms seen;
   Round many western islands have I been
Which bards in fealty to Apollo hold.

We shall have occasion to refer to these different arrangements of rhymes again when we come to deal with individual verse forms, so don't memorize them now unless you are of a mind to.

Rhymes have also been used internally on a line; Blake achieved two master strokes of the pen in that way at the end of "The Garden of Love." If you recall, the poem metaphorically relates the story of someone going to visit an old love who has turned away from life to sterile religion. In the final two lines Blake twice rhymed internally to give the woman's conversion a sense of finality, and he built up to this by leaving the ends of the two previous lines unrhymed. The finality is reinforced by the alliteration of "b"'s and related "v" and "f"'s in key words in the stanza as well as the circularity of walking rounds and binding:

> And I saw it was filled with graves,
> And tomb-stones where flowers should be;
> And Priests in black gowns were walking their rounds,
> And binding with briars my joys & desires.

The partial rhyme of "gowns" and "rounds" is like a crack in a bell, and the association of Jesus' crown of thorns with the binding of joys and desires gives an added note of irony.

WORD AND PHRASE RHYMING: MORE ECHOES-OES

The repetition of words and groups of words is actually another form of rhyming since that too produces an echo-like effect; the echo is simply longer, that's all.

Where repeating single words is concerned, there is no better example than Edgar Allan Poe's celebrated poem "The Bells," which begins—

> Hear the sledges with the bells—
>   Silver bells!
> What a world of merriment their melody foretells!
> How they tinkle, tinkle, tinkle,
>   In the icy air of night!
> While the stars that oversprinkle
> All the heavens, seem to twinkle
>   With a crystalline delight;
>   Keeping time, time, time,
>   In a sort of Runic rhyme,
> To the tintinnabulation that so musically wells
>   From the bells, bells, bells, bells,
>   Bells, bells, bells—
> From the jingling and the tinkling of the bells.

There is no point in belaboring the matter, is there? If you didn't hear anything by the end of this stanza, consider that you may have a tin ear. And imagine what the rest of the poem is like—there are four more lon-ong stanzas!

One thing that you should always remember when it comes to word repetition is that it must be purposeful, which means that everyone—but especially the novice writer—must go over and over his or her work and ruthlessly weed out any unintended repeating of verbiage.

EXERCISE 8

Exaggerated as it is, "The Bells" is another fun poem that one can no more take seriously than "Uppon a Deedmans Hed." So think of some specialized sound that everyone is familiar with, like an alarm clock going off or a doorbell ringing, and see if you can come up with an imitation—including, of course, one or more word or phrase repetitions.

There are several specialized forms of single word repetition, among them the use of the same word or group of words at the ends of successive phrases or clauses (epistrophe)—as in St. Paul's famous statement in I Corinthians:

When I was a child, I spake as a child, I understood as a child, I thought as a child: but when I became a man, I put away childish things.

A favorite ploy of speechmakers past and present is to repeat a word or group of words at the beginnings of successive phrases or clauses (anaphora). The opening section of the first chapter of Genesis makes particularly effective use of this form of word-rhyming together with that above:

In the beginning God created the heaven and the earth.
And the earth was without form, and void; and darkness *was* upon the face of the deep. And the Spirit of God moved upon the face of the waters.
And God said, Let there be light: and there was light.
And God saw the light, that *it was* good: and God divided the light from the darkness.
And God called the light Day, and the darkness he called Night. And the evening and the morning were the first day.

The use of "and" at the beginnings of clauses can be found throughout the Old Testament, but here with the terminal repetition of "light" and "day" it works especially well.

EXERCISE 9

Write a passage in imitation of the one above in which you depict God creating something else. Note: For this you might want to look over the rest of Genesis I to find something that was not specifically mentioned.

Another specialized kind of word-repetition is to use different forms of the same word in a passage or else words that come from the same root (polyptoton), as Shakespeare did three times in this pair of lines from *Troilus and Cressida*:

The Greeks are strong and skillful to their strength,
Fierce to their skill, and to their fierceness valiant;

Which brings us almost back to puns.

EXERCISE 10

Think of three adjectives that one could apply, say, to a favorite sports team, and work up a short descriptive passage using different forms of them.
Psst! Refrain from punning if you can.

Just as a single word or phrase can be repeated to effect, so too can a whole line or a group of lines, in which case it is called a refrain. "Merrily, Merrily, to welcome in the Year" and its variant in Blake's "Spring" is such a refrain, as we have seen.

EXERCISE 11

Take some poem that you have written and try out a number of the lines as refrains. Which one works best? Why? If nothing works and/or you don't want to use one of your poems or don't have any yet, just make up some lines that sound as if they might make interesting refrains.
P.S. Don't be surprised if this turns into a poem. Sometimes it happens that way.

Surely the all-time best-known use of a refrain occurs in Marc bxAntony's Funeral Oration for Caesar in Shakespeare's *Julius Caesar*, where each successive repetition that Caesar was ambitious and Brutus an honorable man serves to convince the audience that the situation was otherwise:

Friends, Romans, countrymen, lend me your ears.
I come to bury Caesar, not to praise him.
The evil that men do lives after them;
The good is oft interréd with their bones.
So let it be with Caesar. The noble Brutus
Hath told you Caesar was ambitious.

If it were so, it was a grievous fault,
And grievously hath Caesar answer'd it.
Here, under leave of Brutus and the rest—
For Brutus is an honorable man;
So are they all, all honorable men—
Come I to speak in Caesar's funeral.
He was my friend, faithful and just to me;
But Brutus says he was ambitious,
And Brutus is an honorable man.
He hath brought many captives home to Rome,
Whose ransoms did the general coffers fill.
Did this in Caesar seem ambitious?
When that the poor have cried, Caesar hath wept;
Ambition should be made of sterner stuff.
Yet Brutus says he was ambitious,
And Brutus is an honorable man.
You all did see that on the Lupercal
I thrice presented him a kingly crown,
Which he did thrice refuse. Was this ambition?
Yet Brutus says he was ambitious,
And, sure, he is an honorable man.
I speak not to disprove what Brutus spoke,
But here I am to speak what I do know.
You all did love him once, not without cause.
What cause withholds you then, to mourn for him?
O judgment! Thou art fled to brutish beasts,
And men have lost their reason. Bear with me;
My heart is in the coffin there with Caesar,
And I must pause till it come back to me.

This passage really bears close scrutiny. Give it that, noting other repetitions of words. Can anyone find a pun on the name Brutus? Don't all answer at once.

EXERCISE 12

Write a speech outlining the shortcomings of someone in political office, or perhaps some official at your college—and, of course, make use of repetition at the beginnings or ends of successive sentences. Do it in prose to give yourself the best practice with this form of repetition. But don't hesitate to use partial rhyme where it seems appropriate.

Before we leave this subject of word and phrase repetition, I should point out that there are any number of long works in which words and phrases are deliberately repeated over and over much as a leitmotif in opera or snatches of a theme song in a Broadway musical. Shakespeare in particular was adept at this, often repeating to keep reminding his audience of the real subject of a particular play lest they be distracted by digressions. *Julius Caesar* is a good case in point—"honor" and its cousin "honest" as well as "noble" are sounded again and again throughout the five acts. And most importantly, so too is "all," beginning with the opening scene where a cobbler and a tribune bandy words over it and its homonym "awl." After a steady stream of "all"'s, a high point comes in the Funeral Oration when Antony indicates where Brutus' knife penetrated Caesar's mantle and cries out, "This was the most unkindest cut of all." The continued repetition of "all" to the bitter end, when justice catches up with the assassins, is there to remind us of that cut—and that the whole of society, from the honorable men who tolerated the act to the ever-fickle rabble, was guilty.

Shakespeare surpassed himself with theme-words later in his career in *Macbeth*, whose end-lines like those of *Julius Caesar* and the other plays are largely unrhymed, as we said. Having killed the King, Macbeth is full of remorse, which Lady Macbeth tries to assuage by telling him, "What's done cannot be undone." The whole play, it turns out, is full of reminders of this statement—for not only are "done" and "do" frequently used, but there are all kinds of internal rhymes with them, including "won," "sun," "minion," "double," "bubble," "rump," "thumb," "come," "drum," "due," "duties," "dues," "undone," "dunnest," "masterdom," "trumpet-tongued," "ambition," "none," "undaunted," "summons," "unrule," "downy," "unbecoming," "anon," "scorpions," "down," "overcome," "summer's," "wonder," "son," "gone," "Acheron," "fool," "cool," "wren," and "run," not to mention the names of the murdered King and his family—Duncan, Malcolm, Donalbain. Indeed the two sounds "un" and "oo" are like drumbeats running through the play—and what do you know, *Macbeth* ends on the rhyme of "one" and "Scone."

So much for rhyming—a few words remain to be said about other matters relating to sound in poetry.

Something different: sound effects

When I was an undergraduate, a fad word that one heard quite often with respect to poetry was *onomatopoeia*, the use of a verbal expression to picture a sound—it almost seemed at times that this was all poetry was about. So that is why this tool occupies such a modest place here.

Actually we are constantly employing *onomatopoeia* in our daily lives, as our many sound-picturing verbs testify—"hiss," "slam," "whirr," and "sizzle" being but a few. In poetry, the word "buzz" is crucial in Emily Dickinson's "I Heard a Fly Buzz When I Died," echoing the buzzing sound for us. But top honors really go once more to Shakespeare for episodes like the Heath Scene in *King Lear*, where the harsh sounds of the words that old, mad Lear chokes out—like "crack," "rage," "cataracts," "hurricanoes," "spout," "drenched," "drowned," "cocks," and so on echo the storm within him as well as that without in the harsh world:

> Blow, winds, and crack your cheeks! Rage, blow!
> You cataracts and hurricanoes, spout
> Till you have drench'd our steeples, drown'd the cocks!
> You sulph'rous and thought-executing fires,
> Vaunt-couriers of oak-cleaving thunderbolts,
> Singe my white head! And thou, all-shaking thunder,
> Strike flat the thick rotundity o' th' world!
> Crack nature's molds, all germains spill at once,
> That makes ingrateful man!

EXERCISE 13

Do you remember that letter of complaint you wrote to a manufacturer about that person's product in Chapter Three? Well, dig it out and look it over—add verbal sound effects to drive home your point. You also wrote (or should have written) an apostrophe or address to the thing itself—if you wish to add the sound effects there instead, by all means do it.

I cannot resist another example from Shakespeare, this speech of Prospero's from his final play *The Tempest*, in which the king resigns his role as magician—where the very lilt and cadence of it all is suggestive of the waving of a wand:

> Ye elves of hills, brooks, standing lakes, and groves,
> And ye that on the sands with printless foot
> Do chase the ebbing Neptune, and do fly him
> When he comes back; you demi-puppets that
> By moonshine do the green sour ringlets make,
> Whereof the ewe not bites; and you whose pastime
> Is to make midnight mushrooms, that rejoice
> To hear the solemn curfew; by whose aid,
> Weak masters though ye be, I have bedimm'd
> The noontide sun, call'd forth the mutinous winds,
> And 'twixt the green sea and the azur'd vault

Set roaring war; to the dread rattling thunder
Have I given fire, and rifted Jove's stout oak
With his own bolt; the strong-bas'd promontory
Have I made shake, and by the spurs pluck'd up
The pine and cedar; graves at my command
Have wak'd their sleepers, op'd, and let 'em forth
By my so potent art. But this rough magic
I here abjure, and, when I have requir'd
Some heavenly music, which even now I do,
To work mine end upon their senses that
This airy charm is for, I'll break my staff,
Bury it certain fathoms in the earth,
And deeper than did ever plummet sound
I'll drown my book.

THOUGHT RHYMING: MORE—MORE ECHOES-OES

What is the repetition of an idea but another form of rhyming, more subtle yet, creating echoes of another kind—like the motions of a distant planet? We have seen how Shakespeare kept his audience's mind on the matter at hand by repeating words and similar sounds; elsewhere he did much the same without reference to sound, for instance in *Hamlet* with the constant repetition of "reason" and other words relating to sanity and madness.

EXERCISE 14

Look back over your own pieces of writing, both in prose and verse, and see if you can find an echoing or prevailing idea. If you can't, would it improve the work to insert one? Try it, employing synonyms and deliberately avoiding sound repetition.

Another mode of thought-echoing is to rephrase a statement using the same grammatical structure. Technically known as parallelism, it was the mainstay of the composers of the Old Testament Psalms, and occurred in three different forms:

1. Where the sense of the first statement is repeated practically verbatim in the second (synonymous)—for example, "At thy rebuke they fled; at the voice of thy thunder they hasted away."
2. In which the second statement represents a progression from or consequence of the first (synthetic)—as in, "They give drink to every beast of the field; the wild asses quench their thirst."

3. Involving a second statement that contradicts or is antithetical to the first (antithetical)—"For the Lord knoweth the way of the righteous: but the way of the ungodly shall perish."

EXERCISE 15

With the above as models, try creating a parallelism of each kind, using as a departure point an event in the news of late.

Some portions of the Old Testament, like this familiar one attributed to Deutero-Isaiah, are notable for their climactic or stair-like building of parallel statements:

He giveth power to the faint; and to *them that have* no might he increaseth strength.

Even the youths shall faint and be weary, and the young men shall utterly fall:

But they that wait upon the Lord shall renew *their* strength; they shall mount up with wings as eagles; they shall run, and not be weary; *and* they shall walk, and not faint.

The first two paragraphs are examples of synonymous parallelism; the third paragraph (beginning with "But") is in opposition to them, and so is in entirety an example of antithetical parallelism. Within the third paragraph, "they shall mount up with wings as eagles" is also synonymous, while the last two statements are consequences of the first two statements, hence examples of synthetic parallelism.

There is one Psalm at least—the Twenty-third—that is made up from beginning to end of smaller and greater parallel units. See if you can sort it out for yourself:

The LORD *is* my shepherd; I shall not want.

He maketh me to lie down in green pastures: He leadeth me beside the still waters.

He restoreth my soul: he leadeth me in the paths of righteousness for his name's sake.

Yea, though I walk through the valley of the shadow of death, I will fear no evil: for Thou *art* with me; Thy rod and Thy staff they comfort me.

Thou preparest a table before me in the presence of mine enemies: Thou anointest my head with oil; my cup runneth over.

Surely goodness and mercy shall follow me all the days of my life: and I will dwell in the house of the LORD for ever.

Now note how effective parallelism can be in the hands of a modern master like Whitman:

A noiseless patient spider,
I mark'd where on a little promontory it stood isolated,
Mark'd how to explore the vacant vast surrounding,
It launch'd forth filament, filament, filament, out of itself,
Ever unreeling them, ever tirelessly speeding them.

And you O my soul where you stand,
Surrounded, detached, in measureless oceans of space,
Ceaselessly musing, venturing, throwing, seeking the spheres to
    connect them,
Till the bridge you will need be form'd, till the ductile anchor hold,
Till the gossamer thread you fling catch somewhere, O my soul.

EXERCISE 16

Take some poem or short prose piece of yours and try extending it
with some parallel statements. If it doesn't pan out, a poem in imitation
of "A Noiseless Patient Spider" is certainly in order.

CHAPTER SIX

The writing of traditional English verse: major forms

It is time now to pick up the thread and put together the main principles of the last two chapters. As I said, most traditional English verse is iambic, and a good deal of that is iambic pentameter, both unrhymed, which is called blank verse and written in paragraphs, and rhymed, which occurs in a variety of formats. In this chapter we will be trying our hands at each, beginning with blank verse and progressing by easy (or uneasy) stages, with examples and student samples, to heroic (iambic pentameter) couplets, then to the elegiac quatrain, a cross-rhymed four-lined iambic pentameter stanza, and finally to the Shakespearian or English sonnet, which is made up of three of those quatrains followed by a couplet.

The object both in this chapter and the next, in which there will be a smorgasbord of other forms, is that the student warm up for free verse, to be covered in Chapter Eight, which represents a reaction against the rules and regulations of tradition. However, should you become enamored of one or more or all of the old forms for their own sake, there's nothing wrong with that either—just so long as you realize that by writing in couplets, for instance, you will be out of synch with your time.

Some preliminaries concerning iambic pentameter (and iambic verse in general)

In Chapter Four, when we were learning (or re-learning) scansion, we dealt largely with lines that scanned out perfectly, but if you recall, in the end, I warned against assuming that a group of those lines constituted good verse. Before launching into particulars, we should address ourselves to that matter.

Let me state a general principle. The best passages in iambic pentameter by all the great writers were quite irregular, with the perfect lines few and far between. To see what I mean, let's consider these lines by George Gascoigne (1525–77) from *The Steel Glas*, a long satirical poem in which he held a steel glass or mirror up to the aristocracy of his day:

And yet therin, I pray you (my good priests)
Pray stil for me, and for my Glasse of steele
That it (nor I) do any minde offend,
Because we shew, all colours in their kinde.
And pray for me, that (since my hap is such
To see men so) I may perceive myselfe.
O worthy words, to ende my worthlesse verse,
Pray for me Priests, I pray you pray for me.

A simple reading is enough, isn't it? It's boring. And why? Because the one thing that good iambic verse—especially iambic pentameter verse, and most especially that of the unrhymed variety—should *not* do when you're reading it is bump up and down like that as if with a bouncing ball.

Now let's look at the same number of lines from Antony's Funeral Oration:

Friends, Romans, countrymen, lend me your ears.
I come to bury Caesar, not to praise him.
The evil that men do lives after them;
The good is oft interréd with their bones.
So let it be with Caesar. The noble Brutus
Hath told you Caesar was ambitious.
If it were so, it was a grievous fault,
And grievously hath Caesar answer'd it.

The difference between bad and good blank verse should strike one at once, again after a single reading.

Shakespeare's lines were irregular then. However, if you scanned those above, you would find that they are irregular only to a point; of the eight lines, three are perfect and two of the others consist of ten syllables. In other words, he wrote with that perfect line in mind, creating variation upon variation, but every now and then, where it seemed "right," he included one or more of those perfect lines.

Did Shakespeare have a set of rules then? No, is the answer. With the object in mind of making his verse conform to speech, he simply let his sensibility and ear guide him; rules came much later, extrapolated from his practices and that of the other great practitioners of iambic pentameter.

Here is what those latter-day experts came up with:

1. The number of syllables per line, normally ten, could be varied to as few as nine, sometimes eight when a point warranted it, and as many as twelve, but never to fewer or more than that. To use "Friends, Romans" as an example, line two consists of eleven syllables, line five of twelve, and line six of nine.

2. Other feet—anapests ($\smile \smile \diagup$), trochees ($\diagup \smile$), dactyls ($\diagup \smile \smile$) —could be used in place of the iamb, as well as two strong stresses in a row (spondee $\diagup \diagup$) and two weak ones (pyrrhic $\smile \smile$)—but not in so wholesale a fashion as to obscure the iamb. Again to use "Friends, Romans" above, most of the feet are iambic, but here and there is something else; for instance on the seventh line, the second foot and possibly the last are pyrrhics or feet consisting of two unaccented syllables:

And griev-/ ous-ly/ hath Cae-/ sar answ-/ er'd it.

3. Instead of a pause at the end of each line (known as end-stopping), one could run the sense or a syntactical unit on to the next line (called enjambment)—however, never to the point of destroying line unity completely. Shakespeare did this with the fifth and sixth lines: "The noble Brutus/ Hath told you Caesar was ambitious."

4. This final rule has to do with something that we have not touched on as yet, pauses within the line (caesuras, indicated in scansion by //). Most perfect iambic pentameter lines tend to have a pause after the second foot (or fourth syllable), even when there is no punctuation to indicate one; in case you're interested, scholars like Northrop Frye in his *Anatomy of Criticism* claim that it is a hangover from that long pause in mid-line in Anglo-Saxon verse. Certainly one can hear it in our old friend, "When I have fears// that I may cease to be"; Shakespeare marked such a pause on the seventh line, "If it were so,// it was a grievous fault." Anyway, the rule regarding good iambic pentameter verse was that the place of the internal pause or caesura could be varied on the line—and it was usually shifted to after the first or third foot. In "Friends, Romans," note the late pauses on the second and fifth lines above. Another possibility, where sense and sensibility dictated it, the number of caesuras per line could be varied as well. Notable in this respect is obviously the first line of "Friends, Romans" with its three pauses.

EXERCISE 1

A full scansion of both of the above passages with caesuras and enjambments (marked with "enj.") is in order here so that the difference between them in quality becomes crystal clear.

If you're in a class, don't be surprised if you all don't come out with exactly the same analyses. Just remember the important thing—that you readily see the difference between the two passages in quality:

And yet/ ther-in,// I pray/ you (my/ good priests)

or

And yet/ ther-in,// I pray/ you/ (my good priests)

Pray still/ for me,// and for/ my Glasse/ of steele
That it/ (nor I)// do an-/ y minde/ of-fend,
Be-cause/ we shew,// all co-/ lours in/ their kinde.
And pray/ for me,// that (since/ my hap/ is such (enj.)
To see/ men so,// I may/ per-ceive/ my-selfe.
O wor-/ thy words,// to ende/ my worth/lesse verse,
Pray for/ me Priests,// I pray/ you pray/ for me.

Friends,// Ro-mans,// coun-try-men,// lend me/ your ears.
I come/ to bu-/ry Cae-/ sar,// not to/ praise him.
The ev-/ il that/ men do/ lives af-/ ter them;
The good/ is oft/ in-ter-/ red with/ their bones.
So let it be/ with Cae-/ sar.// The no-/ blé Bru-/ tus (enj.)
Hath told/ you Cae-/ sar was/ am-bi-/ tious.
If it/ were so,// it was// a grie/ vous fault,
And grie/ /-vous-ly/ hath Cae-/ sar answ-/ er'd it.

EXERCISE 2

At this point, make sure, to begin with, that you have a good command of the full iambic line. Select one (like "When I have fears that I may cease to be") and repeat it over and over aloud. Sometimes it's helpful to sound or tap out just the beat: ⏑ ´/⏑ ´/⏑ ´/⏑ ´/⏑ ´

The next step should not present a problem.

EXERCISE 3

Write a perfect line, a kind of companion to "When I have fears that I may cease to be"—and don't worry about sense at this point. The beat is what we're after.

Do sound and tap this line out to make sure that it's correct. And if you have trouble, keep working at it or create some more perfect lines.

Now for variations.

EXERCISE 4

It usually helps to work only with sounds like bum-bum or da-da. If you're alone and need a "way in," use the pattern of one of the irregular lines in "Friends, Romans" for starters. If you're in a class, you can make a game of creating variations of the basic pattern, going round the room with each student trying to one-up the one before. See how many variations you can come up with—but be sure to stay within the parameters outlined above. For instance, there should be no lines without units of light-heavy—otherwise what you do ceases to be iambic. Every half dozen variations or so, someone (like your instructor) should repeat the basic pattern as a reminder.

Hey, hey, we seem to have gotten away from words, haven't we? We seem to be working with pure sound, doing something akin to creating music. Well, that's what the traditional English poets were doing in part. In fact, for the information of those who decry the fact that England never produced anyone in music on a par with Bach and Mozart—those poets were England's great musical composers.

EXERCISE 5

Write an imperfect line as a second line to one of your perfect lines; keep it unrhymed. If you feel like it, keep on going, and write some more lines of variation.

Before we go on, check, using the guidelines above, to make sure that what you have is not too far out—we don't want to lose sight of iambic pentameter so fast, do we?

Ready? Here we go.

Blank verse

Well, if what you came up with in this last exercise was unrhymed as I suggested, you've begun writing blank verse. All that is needed now is some broadening and deepening.

Just when did unrhymed iambic pentameter or blank verse arise, you may be asking. How soon after Chaucer's success with couplets in *The Canterbury Tales* (ca. 1380's)? No one knows for sure; certainly there was considerable experimenting in English poetic circles for the next century or so—and if you're inquisitive about that period, take a look in George Saintsbury's *History of English Prosody*. What seems clear is that by the early part of the sixteenth century there was a general tendency to drop rhyme; then in the 1550's came the work credited with being the first in true blank verse, a translation of several books of Virgil's *Aeneid* by Henry Howard, the Earl of Surrey.

What the new form needed after that was some strong impetus, which it soon got from the Elizabethan stage, whose audience had an insatiable appetite for blood-and-thunder doings or rip-roaring comedy in verse. And then? Why then came Marlowe (1564–93) and the Bard himself (1564–1616).

Shakespeare's career spanned three decades; during that time he authored thirty-odd plays. While the blank verse in which they were largely written underwent certain changes in conformity with changing public taste, there was a general consistency to it, early and late. Hamlet's all-too-famous "To Be or Not To Be" soliloquy is representative of Shakespeare's blank verse at mid-career. Let it serve as an example of blank verse intended to be spoken and heard on a stage, or dramatic blank verse:

> To be, or not to be, that is the question:
> Whether 'tis nobler in the mind to suffer
> The slings and arrows of outrageous fortune,
> Or to take arms against a sea of troubles,
> And by opposing end them. To die, to sleep—
> No more—and by a sleep to say we end
> The heart-ache and the thousand natural shocks
> That flesh is heir to. 'Tis a consummation
> Devoutly to be wish'd. To die, to sleep;
> To sleep, perchance to dream. Ay, there's the rub,
> For in that sleep of death what dreams may come
> When we have shuffled off this mortal coil,
> Must give us pause. There's the respect
> That makes calamity of so long life.
> For who would bear the whips and scorns of time,
> Th' oppressor's wrong, the proud man's contumely,
> The pangs of despis'd love, the law's delay,
> The insolence of office, and the spurns
> That patient merit of th'unworthy takes,
> When he himself might his quietus make
> With a bare bodkin? Who would fardels bear,
> To grunt and sweat under a weary life,
> But that the dread of something after death,
> The undiscover'd country from whose bourn
> No traveler returns, puzzles the will,

And makes us rather bear those ills we have
Than fly to others that we know not of?
Thus conscience does make cowards of us all;
And thus the native hue of resolution
Is sicklied o'er with the pale cast of thought,
And enterprises of great pitch and moment
With this regard their currents turn awry,
And lose the name of action.

EXERCISE 6

Do a complete scansion of the first fifteen lines of "To Be or Not to Be" (to "long life"), all of them if you feel ambitious, although this isn't necessary.

You should have found the four features of good iambic pentameter given above, including fewer or more than ten syllables per line, the substitution of other feet, enjambment, and variation of the internal pause or caesura and the number of them on a line. In addition, you should have noted one feature at least that is distinctive to Shakespeare—an eleven-syllable line with the extra syllable, a lightly stressed one, coming at the very end of it, the result of his placing polysyllabic words there. If you did not note this mannerism, go back over your scansion and do so now.

I'm sure you've guessed what's coming next and are braced. But before we go on to it, take heart from this response to Hamlet's soul searching by my student Lisa Baroz:

LIFE'S INTRICATE BLESSINGS

No, it is not death of which I speak,
But life and all its blessings bountiful.
Intricate and yet unnoticed in their midst—
For man's ambition clouds his wisest way.
The most essential blessing is of life,
Which carries man upon a magic ride
Through time to future destiny unknown.
Nature, with savage threats of winter storms,
Enfolds the earth with cloaks of purest white.
The sunshine brings new growth within each spring—
Kaleidoscopic colors daily bloom,
And satin clouds wake up to greet the day.
The joy of life abounds in all the fields.
Who can express a mother's joy at birth?

Of newborn's innocence, ecstatic love,
And father's joy of holding his new child.
Of all life's blessed moments shared with joy,
The clock of time will cast them soon away.
Thus, wisdom must replace a man's neglect,
For blessings in themselves are lost in haste.

You see, it can be done.

EXERCISE 7

Now it's your turn to write some dramatic blank verse. Think in terms of a poem of comparable length. May I suggest that you use the speech that you wrote about some official's shortcomings in Chapter Five as a basis—that, or respond to Hamlet with something about the blessings of "being."

Note: sometimes it helps for students to memorize a Shakespearian speech beforehand, and you have a number here in this book to choose from. But above all, whatever you do, when you write dramatic blank verse (or for that matter any other kind), don't try to follow the rules. Simply write as Shakespeare and Marlowe did, with that perfect line in mind.

John Milton (1608–74), our next great practitioner of blank verse, wanted to write for the stage, but in 1642 the London theatres were closed by order of the Puritans, the party to which he belonged, and when they re-opened after the Restoration in 1660, it was to provide fare for a worldly audience that he was utterly out of sympathy with. Added to that, he was blind by then and virtually under house arrest. So what was there to do but as he did—write his masterpiece *Paradise Lost* to be read, in the literary tradition of Virgil. And this plus a nature far more bookish than Shakespeare's made for a blank verse with quite a different texture, which today is labeled epic blank verse.

Consider the opening to that extraordinary work of his:

Of Man's First Disobedience, and the Fruit
Of that Forbidden Tree, whose mortal taste
Brought Death into the World, and all our woe,
With loss of *Eden*, till one greater Man
Restore us, and regain the blissful Seat,
Sing Heav'nly Muse, that on the secret top
Of *Oreb*, or of *Sinai*, didst inspire
That Shepherd, who first taught the chosen Seed,
In the Beginning how the Heav'ns and Earth
Rose out of *Chaos*: Or if *Sion* Hill

Delight thee more, and *Siloa's* Brook that flow'd
Fast by the Oracle of God; I thence
Invoke thy aid to my advent'rous Song,
That with no middle flight intends to soar
Above th' *Aonian* Mount, while it pursues
Things unattempted yet in Prose or Rhyme.
And chiefly Thou O Spirit, that dost prefer
Before all Temples th'upright heart and pure,
Instruct me, for Thou know'st; Thou from the first
Wast present, and with mighty wings outspread
Dove-like satst brooding on the vast Abyss
And mad'st it pregnant: What in me is dark
Illumine, what is low raise and support;
That to the highth of this great Argument
I may assert Eternal Providence,
And justify the ways of God to men.

Note the curious Latin-like syntactic features, like Milton's placing a noun between two adjectives ("the upright heart and pure") and a verb between two subjects ("Or if *Sion* hill/ Delight thee more, and *Siloa's* brook"). How different this is from Shakespeare, is it not?

But that's not all.

EXERCISE 8

What else? Do a full scansion of this selection from *Paradise Lost* to the first full stop ("Rhyme").

Like before with "To Be or Not To Be," you should have found the whole gamut of variations, but not that eleven-syllable line with the light stress at the end, which is distinctively Shakespearian. One feature besides Milton's bookish diction and Latin-like syntax should stand out for you, Milton's mannerism, if you will—his use of consecutive enjambments and more caesuras. This is armchair blank verse—so many lines run on one after another, even with pauses in their midst, would not work well on a stage.

What do you think, do you feel up to it? My student Cynthia Sammarco was:

THE WONDER OF THE WORLD

In the mighty universe Man is born weak
And fragile; he suckles at his mother's

Breasts and struggles to crawl before he walks—
On wings of eagles he climbs the Olympian
Heights. Behold him, O Zeus, in all his glory,
How wonderful he is. He smites your
Thunderbolts with his slingshot. Beware!
He will not be deterred. He has a new
God, one who is not as frightening as
You, but infinitely more powerful.

EXERCISE 9

Again, may I recommend memorization of this or another passage of
Paradise Lost first. Then try for ten or so lines, remembering those successive enjambments and mid-line pauses. Be careful, though, of the
Latinate vocabulary and sentence structure—too much of that will result
in an unintentional parody. As for subject matter, take your pick. Since
Milton wrote extensively of his blindness elsewhere in *Paradise Lost,*
you might consider dwelling on one of your own problems or handi-
caps.

After Milton, blank verse became a secondary form, giving way to
the rhymed iambic pentameter couplet, which became pre-eminent in
the hands of Dryden and Pope. But in the late eighteenth century it
experienced a revival—first and foremost in the hands of William
Wordsworth (1770–1850), who used it for his ode "Tintern Abbey"
and a long spiritual autobiography in epic form, posthumously titled
The Prelude, which he worked on during most of his active years.

We've already had a taste of both works, you will recall. Here is
another from *The Prelude*, one of the high points, where Wordsworth
spoke of crossing the Alps on foot as a young man. Notice how the
poet, a master at his craft, built up to the climax at the end with
parallel statement after parallel statement—as if keeping pace with the
climb—

. . . The immeasurable height
Of woods decaying, never to be decayed,
The stationary blasts of waterfalls,
And in the narrow rent at every turn
Winds thwarting winds, bewildered and forlorn,
The torrents shooting from the clear blue sky,
The rocks that muttered close upon our ears,
Black drizzling crags that spake by the way-side
As if a voice were in them, the sick sight
And giddy prospect of the raving stream,

> The unfettered clouds and region of the Heavens,
> Tumult and peace, the darkness and the light—
> Were all like workings of one mind, the features
> Of the same face, blossoms upon one tree;
> Characters of the great Apocalypse,
> The types and symbols of Eternity,
> Of first, and last, and midst, and without end.

The marvelous staccato-like effect achieved with multiple caesuras in the last line was an old Miltonic trick—as for instance, when Satan on escaping from Hell in *Paradise Lost* "O'er bog or steep, through strait, rough, dense, or rare,/ With head, hands, wings, or feet pursues his way,/ And swims or sinks, or wades, or creeps, or flies." But unlike Milton, Wordsworth worked up to his staccatos by deliberately being very sparing with caesuras in the verse paragraph until that last line.

EXERCISE 10

It would not hurt to scan this passage too. The question that you should ask yourself is not how Wordsworth further resembles Milton or is like Shakespeare here, but in what way or ways he is uniquely himself.

Before we leave blank verse, a final word remains to be said about sound echoes—for just because this verse form has no end-rhyme does not mean that there are no sound correspondences. We must just look for the subtler ones—alliteration, assonance, consonance, etc.

EXERCISE 11

Do so in the three examples of blank verse by Shakespeare, Milton, and Wordsworth. To what extent do echoes, great and small, onomatopoeia, and parallelism contribute to the total effect in each case?

When you are finished, go back to your own two efforts in blank verse and review, and if it so moves you, revise accordingly.

Are you ready to go the limit with blank verse?

EXERCISE 12

Here's a choice: take the best of your two pieces of blank verse and work it over, or write a new poem in blank verse entirely in your own voice.

My student Michael Toro offered this:

LOVERS WITHIN THE DARKNESS

The city sleeps beneath a neon moon,
Glowing within: a dreamland entwining.

The two of us, she and I, imbued erotic;
Floods of night pour in through our window:
Reveal eyes that glimmer to glaring street lights,
From blood pulsating to motion in our loins;
In time to mouths compressed in nectars stirred within,
Our shadows cast a storm of torrid visions.
Profound embrace: our flesh ignites incessant flames—
Unites our spirits—tempestuous oceans;
Our bodies awash, ablaze, in waves enfolding,
Beads of sweat cascade in passion's rain;
The flow of city lights gleams and swirls upon us,
Our hearts beat as one in frenzied rhythm;
We merge transfigured through chasms:
The brink begins to shine in the Eastern sky,
We thrust in rays of Mars and Venus soaring
Before the sun a wonder bursting a-glow,
As this night's embrace unwraps the dawn.

ONE STEP—THE HEROIC COUPLET

Iambic pentameter couplets date back to Chaucer as has been indicated. But their heyday came much later with Dryden (1631–1700) and Pope (1688–1744), who began by translating parts of the *Aeneid* and *Iliad* into them (hence the name heroic couplet), and who ended by using them as vehicles for their own work. Alas, this was largely given over to satirizing contemporary politics and related matters, and thus makes for very dull reading nowadays unless one is particularly interested in the finer points of seventeenth-century political satire. For example, in *Absalom and Achitophel*, Dryden made use of the Bible to suggest how the Earl of Shaftesbury (Achitophel, one of King David's followers) was tempting the young Duke of Monmouth, Charles II's illegitimate son (Absalom, a son of David) to rebel. But today we could not care less about either story; indeed, the only appealing feature may be Dryden's cute and clever mode of telling. See for yourself, here's the opening:

In pious times, ere priestcraft did begin,
Before polygamy was made a sin;
When man on many multiplied his kind,
Ere one to one was cursedly confined;
When nature prompted and no law denied
Promiscuous use of concubine and bride;
Then Israel's monarch after Heaven's own heart,

His vigorous warmth did variously impart
To wive and slaves; and, wide as his command,
Scattered his Maker's image through the land.
Michal, of royal blood, the crown did wear,
A soil ungrateful to the tiller's care:
Not so the rest; for several mothers bore
To godlike David several sons before.
But since like slaves his bed they did ascend,
No true succession could their seed attend.
Of all this numerous progeny was none
So beautiful, so brave, as Absalom.

One distinct difference between Chaucer's couplets and these above should have become apparent to you: Dryden's tend to be self-contained units, or closed, as we say. You will soon become aware of other differences.

Of the two later masters of the latter day or heroic couplet, Pope was clearly the outstanding figure, a Shakespeare to Dryden's Marlowe, and he set the standard for a century of imitators down to Wordsworth and Byron. In conformity with his age—called Augustan or Neo-classical—Pope's couplets are more regular than blank verse, and his rhyme pure. Also, not surprisingly, Pope showed a preference for Latinate words over the colloquial. Let this paragraph from his *Essay on Criticism*, already in part familiar to us, serve as an example:

A *little learning* is a dang'rous thing;
Drink deep, or taste not the Pierian spring.
There shallow draughts intoxicate the brain,
And drinking largely sobers us again.
Fir'd at first sight with what the Muse imparts,
In fearless youth we tempt the heights of Arts,
While from the bounded level of our mind
Short views we take, nor see the lengths behind;
But more advanc'd, behold with strange surprise
New distant scenes of endless science rise!
So pleas'd at first the tow'ring Alps we try,
Mount o'er the vales, and seem to tread the sky,
Th' eternal snows appear already past,
And the first clouds and mountains seem the last;
But, those attain'd, we tremble to survey
The growing labours of the lengthen'd way,
Th' increasing prospects tires our wand'ring eyes,
Hills peep o'er hills, and Alps on Alps arise!

EXERCISE 13

Oh, you've got a lot of work cut out for you here. First of all, do a complete scansion of these lines, remembering that you've already done the first four in Chapter Four. How many perfect lines are there? What sorts of foot substitution did you find, and what about caesuras? Finally, what of the rhymes—what kinds did Pope use?

Pope's modes of variation were thus much the same as those of the writers of blank verse. But that was not all—he also made extensive use of parallelism, together with assonance and consonance, including alliteration and sometimes striking puns, as in "New distant scenes of endless science rise!"

EXERCISE 14

Examine the passage for other instances of parallelism, word repetition, and partial rhyme within the lines.

Pope achieved further variety by the use of three rhymed lines here and there, a triplet in other words, for instance in the following passage from the *Essay*:

> But most by Numbers judge a Poet's song;
> And smooth or rough, with them is right or wrong:
> In the bright Muse though thousand charms conspire,
> Her voice is all these tuneful fools admire;
> Who haunt Parnassus but to please their ear,
> Not mend their minds; as some to Church repair,
> Not for the doctrine, but the music there.

Note how the unity of the couplet ("conspire"/ "admire") before the triplet is broken by the continuation of the sense of the passage to "minds" in the midst of the triplet, and at the same time how the lines are bound together by the repetition of the "ai" sound and the "r," occurring in all the line-ends but the first. And most important, the effect of disrupted normal unity together with a differently achieved one goes hand in hand with the sense.

Pope also occasionally used a six-beat line (iambic hexameter or, as it is known, an alexandrine), and nowhere does he do this more successfully than in the conclusion to the above paragraph. Notice how he anticipated that magnificent final line with its extra foot with "creep," which he reinforced by rhyming with "sleep" and partially rhyming with "needless":

These equal syllables alone require,
Tho' oft the ear the open vowels tire;
While expletives their feeble aid do join;
And ten low words oft creep in one dull line:
While they ring round the same unvary'd chimes,
With sure returns of still expected rhymes;
Where-e'er you find "the cooling western breeze,"
In the next line, it "whispers through the trees:"
If crystal streams "with pleasing murmurs creep,"
The reader's threaten'd (not in vain) with "sleep:"
Then, at the last an only couplet fraught
With some unmeaning thing they call a thought,
A needless Alexandrine ends the song
That, like a wounded snake, drags its slow length along.

And notice how the picture of the snake crawling is bolstered acoustically by the four heavy accents in a row—"drags its slow length"—as well as the alliteration of "s"'s and "l"'s.

Skillful as Pope was at this sort of thing, his main strength lay in short, witty statements—aphorisms, in other words—which are often valued in and of themselves. "A little learning" etc. is one such, the snake simile above another; here are some more, gathered from hither and yon:

True Wit is Nature to advantage dress'd,
What oft was thought, but ne'er so well express'd.

'T is not enough no harshness gives offence,
The sound must seem an Echo to the sense.

Good-nature and good-sense must ever join; (pronounced "jine")
To err is human, to forgive, divine.

Nay, fly to altars; there they'll talk you dead:
For Fools rush in where Angels fear to tread.

Know then thyself, presume not God to scan;
The proper study of Mankind is Man.

EXERCISE 15

Again one has a choice. Either write ten or so lines of heroic couplets including an aphorism, or else dream up two or three aphorisms in couplet form, good ones.

Hint: if you get into trouble, try thinking up rhymes first—with the idea, of course, that in the end all of them might change.

One of my favorite students, Arnold Greissle, who happens to be my husband, brought forth this:

TELL ME WHERE

The trashy city has us by the throat
As to the sky it lifts its smoggy coat:
Above, a mass of grey and lifeless cubes,
Below, a net of trains in dusty tubes.
Graffiti grace the city's crumbling walls,
And homeless shapes lie bundled up in balls—
To find escape from winter's icy bite,
From hunger, drugs, and rape in aimless flight.
We see these lives in hopeless misery spent
And ask ourselves—"Where is our government?"

HOP AND SKIP—THE ELEGIAC QUATRAIN

Now let's consider a four-lined iambic pentameter stanza or quatrain with cross rhymes. Unlike the couplet, this stanza by itself is of relatively recent vintage, made famous by Thomas Gray (1716–71) in his "Elegy Written in a Country Churchyard," which was composed to express sorrow over the death of a close friend but became for the public and remained forever after a lament for what we today would call the common man.

The opening to the "Elegy" tells the whole tale:

The curfew tolls the knell of parting day,
   The lowing herd wind slowly o'er the lea,
The plowman homeward plods his weary way,
   And leaves the world to darkness and to me.

Now fades the glimmering landscape on the sight,
   And all the air a solemn stillness holds,
Save where the beetle wheels his droning flight,
   And drowsy tinklings lull the distant folds;

Save that from yonder ivy-mantled tower
   The moping owl does to the moon complain
Of such, as wandering near her secret bower,
   Molest her ancient solitary reign.

Beneath those rugged elms, that yew tree's shade,
　　Where heaves the turf in many a moldering heap,
Each in his narrow cell forever laid,
　　The rude forefathers of the hamlet sleep.

The breezy call of incense-breathing morn,
　　The swallow twittering from the straw-built shed,
The cock's shrill clarion, or the echoing horn,
　　No more shall rouse them from their lowly bed.

For them no more the blazing hearth shall burn,
　　Or busy housewife ply her evening care;
No children run to lisp their sire's return,
　　Or climb his knees the envied kiss to share.

Oft did the harvest to their sickle yield,
　　Their furrow oft the stubborn glebe has broke;
How jocund did they drive their team afield!
　　How bowed the woods beneath their sturdy stroke!

Let not Ambition mock their useful toil,
　　Their homely joys, and destiny obscure;
Nor Grandeur hear with a disdainful smile
　　The short and simple annals of the poor.

The boast of heraldry, the pomp of power,
　　And all that beauty, all that wealth e'er gave,
Awaits alike the inevitable hour.
　　The paths of glory lead but to the grave.

This being, after all, iambic verse, Gray used some of the same old tricks for achieving variety.

EXERCISE 16

To see this, do a full scansion of the first three stanzas, and note as well the use of word repetition, parallelism, and partial rhyme within the lines.

Did you notice that the quatrains are almost all self-contained? If you didn't, look again now. But how different their texture is from everything that we read of Pope's—the "Elegy" is a lazy river, Pope's couplets vibrant and elastic. What accounts for the difference? Well, one contributing factor, which you would have seen from your scansion, is that in the "Elegy" there are relatively few caesuras, another an overabundant use of parallelism. Beyond that there is Gray's consistently stately diction, together with a predilection for soft sounds, especially "r"'s and "l"'s—liquids, we call them—which you would also have noted in your examination, hopefully. Do read something by Pope aloud and follow it with this passage to hear the difference if it did not strike you at once.

After Gray, the elegiac quatrain enjoyed a long distinguished history down almost until today, reserved always as a medium for sad subjects. Notable among the works in that form was Wordsworth's "Elegiac Stanzas" (1807), subtitled "Suggested by a Picture of Peele Castle, in a Storm, Painted by Sir George Beaumont," which was written in memory of the poet's brother John, victim of a shipwreck.

The opening lines are:

I was thy neighbour once, thou rugged Pile!
Four summer weeks I dwelt in sight of thee:
I saw thee every day; and all the while
Thy Form was sleeping on a glassy sea.

The tone, though sad, is somewhat different from Gray's in the "Elegy"—this is discursive and personal—with caesuras on two of the four lines and the pronoun "I" much in evidence. And so it goes for the rest of the "Elegiac Stanzas" to the finale, when still with the painting of Peele castle in a storm in mind, Wordsworth wrote:

O 'tis a passionate Work!—yet wise and well,
Well chosen is the spirit that is here;
That Hulk which labours in the deadly swell,
This rueful sky, this pageantry of fear!

And this huge Castle, standing here sublime,
I love to see the look with which it braves,
Cased in the unfeeling armour of old time,
The lightning, the fierce wind, and trampling waves.

Farewell, farewell the heart that lives alone,
Housed in a dream, at distance from the Kind!   *mankind*
Such happiness, wherever it be known,
Is to be pitied; for 'tis surely blind.

But welcome fortitude, and patient cheer,
And frequent sights of what is to be borne!
Such sights, or worse, as are before me here.—
Not without hope we suffer and we mourn.

A similarly sad tone pervades Edward Fitzgerald's "Rubáiyát of Omar Khayyám" (composed 1859–79), in which a slightly different rhyme scheme was used, as one can see from this well-known quatrain:

The Moving Finger writes; and, having writ,
Moves on: nor all your Piety nor Wit
   Shall lure it back to cancel half a Line,
Nor all your Tears wash out a Word of it.

A final flowering of the elegiac quatrain occurs in Hart Crane's introduction or "Proem: To Brooklyn Bridge" (1930). Do be sure to take a look at it—you can find it in most standard anthologies. Note Crane's use of cross-rhymes, both full and partial (for example, "sleights"/"scene"/"again"/"screen"), and how he varied this with couplets ("away"/"day") and with quatrains whose line-endings starkly have little or no sound-relationship to one another ("loft"/"parapets"/ "ballooning"/"caravan").

EXERCISE 17

It is difficult to scan "To Brooklyn Bridge" and I'm not sure how productive it would be. But in order to see how careful a workman Hart Crane was, do a syllable count of it by the line at least.

In his restrained use of cross-rhymes, a good number of which were partial, Crane took the elegiac quatrain just about as far as it would go. This is what my student Laura Marie Martino did with it:

FREE

When I have thoughts that I may soon be free,
My eyes become a twilight star above.
But then the darkness covers what I see,
And I become an orphan—no longer loved.

Betrayed by those who wished the life of me,
Where I was shattered with their screams so loud.
They—blinded by my hurt and crying tears,
For they could not rejoice because they're proud.

So I became an orphan of their tree,
Where blame and hurt was put upon my branch.
But as I grow, I know what I shall be—
A growing flower free upon a ranch.

Now it's your turn.

EXERCISE 18

Write a poem consisting of at least three elegiac quatrains. Retain the cross-rhymes throughout, but if you find true rhymes interfering with the sense, don't hesitate to incorporate partial ones.

GETTING IT ALL TOGETHER—THE ENGLISH OR SHAKESPEARIAN SONNET

Finally—we have arrived. The English sonnet, made famous by Shakespeare, consists of three cross-rhymed iambic pentameter quatrains followed by an iambic pentameter couplet. But it must be understood before we go one step further that in the two previous sections of this chapter, the cart was put before the horse—this sonnet and its sister the Petrarchan sonnet (to be covered in the next chapter) were popular long before the elegiac quatrain and the heroic or modern form of the couplet.

The sonnet in both of its versions goes back to Sir Thomas Wyatt (1503–42) and Henry Howard, Earl of Surrey (1517–47). But its history need not concern us here—except to say that Surrey is credited with being the first to use the English type and that by the time Shakespeare arrived on the scene (1564–1616), quite a number of poets had tried their hands at it. In other words, by no means was he Columbus when it came to the sonnet, any more than with blank verse. Rather, he took and worked with what he found, and carried it to new heights—brilliant, beautiful ones—as, for instance, in the following, his Seventy-third Sonnet:

That time of year thou mayst in me behold
When yellow leaves, or none, or few, do hang
Upon those boughs which shake against the cold,
Bare ruin'd choirs, where late the sweet birds sang.
In me thou see'st the twilight of such day
As after sunset fadeth in the west,
Which by and by black night doth take away,
Death's second self, that seals up all in rest.
In me thou see'st the glowing of such fire
That on the ashes of his youth doth lie,

As the death-bed whereon it must expire,
Consum'd with that which it was nourish'd by.
    This thou perceiv'st, which makes thy love more strong,
    To love that well which thou must leave ere long.

What we have here is a long statement presented over the course of the three quatrains—which are nevertheless self-contained—followed by a quick brief statement in the couplet. In the first quatrain the "I" offers a view of himself as being in the late fall of his life. The second and third quatrains are each parallel statements, employing day's end and an expiring fire as the analogy or conceit, as such elaborate metaphors were called in Shakespeare's time. All three quatrains, covertly as well as overtly, share very bright and grim colors, which are more strongly contrasted from one quatrain to the next. And sound, both real and imagined, seems to die away in each in much the same fashion. At the same time the colors are more intensely concentrated, and so too are the rhymes, the "ai" sound connecting all four lines of the third quatrain—"fire"/"lie"/"expire"/"by."

The couplet provides a resolution in the form of a complete reversal—the "thou" loves the "I" that much more because of the situation, and then, as casual as you will, comes: "To love that well which thou must leave ere long." The end-rhyme of the couplet—"strong"/ "long"—nevertheless brings us back to the beginning—"hang"/"sang."

EXERCISE 19

Do a complete scansion of this sonnet. Don't neglect interlinear sound correspondences, and be sure to note repetitions of word, phrase, and thought as well.

No two of Shakespeare's sonnets are alike in strategy; the truth is that he was always careful to fit the sound to the sense, as Pope very wisely counseled a century or so later. For instance, in Shakespeare's Twenty-ninth Sonnet, the first two quatrains are run on, and there are two resolutions—after the end of the third quatrain and with the couplet, the one reinforcing the other like repeated "addio"'s in an Italian opera:

When, in disgrace with fortune and men's eyes,
I all alone beweep my outcast state,
And trouble deaf heaven with my bootless cries,
And look upon myself and curse my fate,
Wishing me like to one more rich in hope,

Featur'd like him, like him with friends possess'd,
Desiring this man's art and that man's scope,
With what I most enjoy contented least;
Yet in these thoughts myself almost despising,
Haply I think on thee, and then my state,
Like to the lark at break of day arising
From sullen earth, sings hymns at heaven's gate;
 For thy sweet love rememb'red such wealth brings
 That then I scorn to change my state with kings.

EXERCISE 20

 Do a scansion of this sonnet as well. Be sure to note words that Shakespeare repeated and the part that they play in unifying the whole.

From both of the foregoing it seems clear that this particular form of the sonnet requires two junctures—one at the end of the second quatrain, the other at the end of the third. The third quatrain is thus in a pivotal position, as a quickener of the first two quatrains and/or anticipator of the couplet.

After Shakespeare, the English sonnet went into a kind of eclipse from which it never really recovered, only this single notable example by John Keats (1795–1821) occurring some two centuries later. The resemblance in strategy to Shakespeare's Seventy-third Sonnet above should be immediately apparent—there are three parallel statements in the three quatrains, and the repetition of the "r" sound in "hour"/ "more"/"power"/"shore" in the final one is certainly reminiscent of what he did in that quatrain, as is the connection between "think" and "sink" and "brain" and "grain" in the couplet and first quatrain:

When I have fears that I may cease to be
 Before my pen has glean'd my teeming brain,
Before high-piléd books, in charact'ry,
 Hold like rich garners the full-ripen'd grain;
When I behold, upon the night's starr'd face,
 Huge cloudy symbols of a high romance,
And think that I may never live to trace
 Their shadows, with the magic hand of chance;
And when I feel, fair creature of an hour!
 That I shall never look upon thee more,
Never have relish in the faery power
 Of unreflecting love!—then on the shore
Of the wide world I stand alone, and think
Till Love and Fame to nothingness do sink.

Note the number of run-ons, especially their occurrence in mid-quatrain on the second and eleventh lines, and how the one on the twelfth line breaks down the final quatrain and adds to the couplet. It's almost as if we are watching the dissolution of this form of the English or Shakespearian sonnet before our very eyes.

EXERCISE 21

Even so, do a thorough scansion of "When I Have Fears" and note parallel statements.

One last word about the English or Shakespearian sonnet—if you will take a look back at our three examples, you will find that in them Shakespeare and Keats were primarily exercising their intellects; yes, fears the "I" of "When I Have Fears" may have begun with, but he ends on a note of thought—"then on the shore/ Of the wide world I stand alone, and *think*/ Till Love and Fame to nothingness do sink." For love and the other emotions we must look to this sonnet's sister form to be covered in the next chapter.

It's time! But first watch what my student Michael Toro did with the English or Shakespearian sonnet.

A FANTASY TO BEYOND

The world's eclipsed behind a veil of dreams,
Our eyes avoid the Sun's reality;
We live our lives in masques, escapist themes,
In shades immortal, we hide in fantasy.
Each day, Destiny beckons us as Its slaves,
To rise to glory, beauty, and jewels.
Each night, Destiny lullabies us to our graves,
With songs of poets, prophets, and fools.
Once I glanced beyond the painted scene,
To glimpse the Truth engraved upon the Sun.
The light was a brilliant, intellectual sheen,
My mind enlightened was forced to run—
To seek illusion beneath my mortal shrouds,
From wizards' sorcery to rainbows in clouds.

EXERCISE 22

Even after all of our build-up, it may be wise to begin gradually with the English or Shakespearian sonnet. May I suggest using the rhymes of one of the samples above and for starters writing fourteen lines of non-sense, including two related quatrains, an additional one that is less related, and a final resolution in a couplet.

How do you feel? Good? Coraggio!

EXERCISE 23

Begin now with an actual English or Shakespearian sonnet. Be liberal with variations, including partial rhyme. Just take care that sound does not jar with sense. For a true Shakespearian flavor, remember that this version of the sonnet is a poem of the head, not the heart—maybe the best way to demonstrate this is to see if you can include a set of analogies or conceits as in the Seventy-third Sonnet. But for this you are going to have to do a lot of legwork with the pen in advance.

My student Karen Laszlo came up with the following on a familiar contemporary scene, and varied the texture of her verse accordingly:

COCONUT GROVE

The night is humid, strung with palm-kissed stars;
Short grasses crunch like crabshells underneath
The breath of nightblooms, colored red, like Mars;
Palmetto rhythms play to faery feet.
Step lightly, gaily, into Tigertails;
'Round velvet couches dipped in red carpet.
Cathedral pieces hide photos of males,
Whose nudity and smiles show no regret.
Imprismed mirrors, artisan bangles,
Capture embraces as heartaches stand tall.
Kisses sigh, their very souls do dangle,
Like dark jeweled studs chained to smooth stucco walls.
Why do we question these epicene teams,
Making love underneath this night of dreams?

CHAPTER SEVEN

The writing of traditional English verse: other forms . . . including exotica

Our treasure-trove of traditional English verse forms is by no means exhausted—indeed even at the end of this chapter there will be many lesser forms that students will want to pursue on their own. So with this understood, let's designate the forms that are covered below the majors of the minors.

WHAT! THE ITALIANS HAVE A SONNET TOO?

Yes, they do—or at least they did. Today it's referred to as the Petrarchan sonnet after the Italian poet Petrarch (1304–74), who composed a whole series of sonnets of that type (or a sonnet sequence, as we would say) to celebrate his love for a woman named Laura. Largely owing to this, sonnets generally came to be associated with love and this Petrarchan or Italian type has been used, by and large, for subjects that are charged with emotion, whereas, as I've intimated, the English or Shakespearian sonnet has usually been an intellectual vehicle.

Likewise consisting of fourteen lines, the Italian or Petrarchan sonnet nevertheless has an entirely different structure. There is an octave consisting of two quatrains with the same rhymes in envelope fashion (abbaabba), in which a problem is stated. And then there is a sestet loosely employing two or three more rhymes, where a solution to the problem is offered. The two greater units—octave and sestet—have been likened to inhaling and exhaling, and the contraction and release of muscles.

Sir Thomas Wyatt (1503–42) is credited with having composed the first Petrarchan or Italian sonnets in English, following a trip to Italy. But because English is not rich in words with similar endings like Italian and other Romance languages, this type was not quick to catch on. John Milton, another lover of things Italian, paved the way a century later with his Petrarchan sonnets. However, as Dr. Johnson pointed out, while Milton was quite capable of chipping a colossus out of rock, he was awkward at carving heads out of cherry stones—and it was to be another century before a true master emerged, William Wordsworth (1770–1850), who, in his lifetime, wrote over five hundred Petrarchan sonnets, a dozen or more of them incomparable. Early on, Wordsworth claimed that he found solace from his personal troubles in the strict requirements of the Petrarchan form—in other words, that he was able to lose himself in those requirements.

In one of his best-known sonnets, "The World is Too Much With Us," a common complaint is registered, indeed one that is *still* with us—we have lost touch with our roots, natural and poetical:

> The world is too much with us; late and soon,
> Getting and spending, we lay waste our powers:
> Little we see in Nature that is ours;
> We have given our hearts away, a sordid boon!
> This Sea that bares her bosom to the moon;
> The winds that will be howling at all hours,
> And are up-gathered now like sleeping flowers;
> For this, for every thing, we are out of tune;
> It moves us not.—Great God! I'd rather be
> A Pagan suckled in a creed outworn;
> So might I, standing on this pleasant lea,
> Have glimpses that would make me less forlorn;
> Have sight of Proteus rising from the sea;
> Or hear old Triton blow his wreathéd horn.

The octave actually laps over into the sestet, "It moves us not" being the last in a series of parallel statements—"we lay waste"; "we have given"; "we are out of tune." At the same time, "It moves us not" is in itself "out of tune" with those statements, all beginning with "we" as they do, so its function in terms of octave and sestet is pivotal or transitional. The same kind of "dissonance" occurs in the sestet when it comes to parallel statement, with "have glimpses," "have sight of," and then "hear." The sestet is also linked to the octave by the "r" and "n" in the crucial end-rhyme—"outworn,"/"forlorn,"/"horn," which refers us back to the "oon" and "owers" end-rhymes of the octave.

EXERCISE 1

Do a complete scansion of this poem, paying particular attention to echoes of the octave in the sestet as well as contrasts between them.

A generation later John Keats (1795–1821), who admired Shakespeare and Milton as well as Wordsworth, tried his hand once, magnificently, at the Italian or Petrarchan sonnet in "On First Looking into Chapman's Homer." To appreciate fully what he did, it is necessary to be aware that Chapman was a Renaissance translator of Homer—the realms of gold are thus books, and the whole business of traveling is an analogy or conceit for reading:

Much have I travell'd in the realms of gold,
    And many goodly states and kingdoms seen;
    Round many western islands have I been
Which bards in fealty to Apollo hold.
Oft of one wide expanse had I been told
    That deep-brow'd Homer ruled as his demesne;
    Yet did I never breathe its pure serene
Till I heard Chapman speak out loud and bold:
Then felt I like some watcher of the skies
    When a new planet swims into his ken;
Or like stout Cortez when with eagle eyes
    He star'd at the Pacific—and all his men
Look'd at each other with a wild surmise—
    Silent, upon a peak in Darien.

Note the array of parallel statements in the octave—"Much have I travell'd," "Round many western islands have I been," "of one wide expanse had I been told"—and the single echo in the sestet—"Then felt I." Here "Yet did I never breathe" and "Till I heard" act as bridges. Note too the echo of the "een" end-rhyme of the octave in the quintessential "en"-rhyme of "ken"/"men"/"Darien" in the sestet.

EXERCISE 2

Don't neglect to do a full scansion of this poem as well, and by all means compare your results with those of your analysis of "The World is Too Much With Us."

A discussion of the mechanics of the Italian or Petrarchan sonnet, brief though it be, would not be complete without some notice of the famous Forty-third Sonnet by Elizabeth Barrett Browning (1806–61) from her sequence *Sonnets from the Portuguese*:

How do I love thee? Let me count the ways.
I love thee to the depth and breadth and height
My soul can reach, when feeling out of sight
For the ends of Being and ideal Grace.
I love thee to the level of everyday's
Most quiet need, by sun and candle-light.
I love thee freely, as men strive for Right;

I love thee purely, as they turn from Praise.
I love thee with the passion put to use
In my old griefs, and with my childhood's faith.
I love thee with a love I seemed to lose
With my lost saints—I love thee with the breath,
Smiles, tears, of all my life! and, if God choose,
I shall but love thee better after death.

This work always has intensely positive supporters and comparably negative critics. Which are you? Why?

EXERCISE 3

Before you answer, subject the poem to a thorough analysis, making sure to note the poet's use of partial rhyme at the ends of lines and how she nevertheless managed to create a sound echo in the sestet.

One also cannot help mentioning another post-Wordsworthian attempt at the Italian or Petrarchan sonnet, "The Windhover," written by Gerard Manley Hopkins in 1877—which because of its almost total departure from iambic pentameter and use of a single rhyme in the octave (reminding us of our old friend Skelton), might well be called an Italian or Petrarchan anti-sonnet:

I caught this morning morning's minion, king-
    dom of daylight's dauphin, dapple-dawn-drawn Falcon, in his riding
    Of the rolling level underneath him steady air, and striding
High there, how he rung upon the rein of a wimpling wing
In his ecstasy! then off, off forth on swing,
    As a skate's heel sweeps smooth on a bow-bend: the hurl and gliding
    Rebuffed the big wind. My heart in hiding
Stirred for a bird,—the achieve of, the mastery of the thing!

Brute beauty and valour and act, oh, air, pride, plume, here
    Buckle! AND the fire that breaks from thee then, a billion
Times told lovelier, more dangerous, O my chevalier!

    No wonder of it: shéer plód makes plow down sillion   *furrow*
Shine, and blue-bleak embers, ah my dear,
    Fall, gall themselves, and gash gold-vermilion.

Hopkins' syntax certainly is unusual at times, forcing one to guess at his meaning; consider "shéer plód makes plow down sillion" with its accents to indicate stress. How do this statement and other puzzlers contribute to the peculiarly nervous or agitated quality of the poem? And what in turn does that quality do to our perception of the subject?

EXERCISE 4

While you're at it, you might as well scan this poem of Hopkins to discover which lines are in iambic pentameter and how the rhymes work. Question: are there any end-rhymes that are actually partial rhymes?

Elizabeth Barrett Browning and Hopkins must certainly have provided you with some food for thought respecting the Italian or Petrarchan sonnet. But despair not, the real thing can be done by a fledgling poet, and here is living proof by Joedy Lo Presto:

A PSYCHIC PSYCHE'S VOW TO CUPID

As evening softly kills the light of day,
I wait in my chambers until you return.
With pounding heart and quickening pulse I learn
That I desire more of you—please stay!
Are you some monster, I've heard people say,
That your nocturnal visits cause concern?
Morning dawns, I come awake and turn,
To find myself alone—you've gone away.
Should I believe what they profess is true,
And put my left-brain logic to the test?
No! Intuition tells me I am right—
There is no evil lurking inside you.
My body, mind, and spirit know you best;
Six senses pay you homage through the night.

EXERCISE 5

You might want to sneak up on the Petrarchan or Italian sonnet, this most difficult of poetic forms, as we did with the English or Shakespearian sonnet—with rhymes and nonsense lines.

If not, then get to work, bearing in mind that you effort should in some way be emotional. The octave with its two rhymes will present the greatest difficulty, so don't hesitate to use partial rhyme even of the most tenuous kind. As for the sestet, English poets seem to have favored the following schemes: cdcdcd, cdecde, cdeced, cdcdee. But you do as sense and sound dictate—that is, to a point. Using a single sound as Hopkins did in "The Windhover" octave, even if it seems to work, would really be self-defeating for our purposes.

English ballads date back to the Middle Ages, when they were sung to tunes, and for this reason they are generally referred to as folk ballads. While their form varied, all ballads told stories, usually with tragic endings, and sometimes, though not always, involving love. The manner of telling was terse, meaning with few details and abrupt transitions, which made for an impersonal or dead-pan tone. People and things were described with stock epithets (or clichés, as we would say today)—for instance, a maiden's cheeks were red as roses, her brow milk-white. End-rhyme was employed, but there was also a heavy use of alliteration internally; other structural features included refrains and a form of parallelism known as incremental repetition, whereby something was repeated with a slight variation that was important to the story.

The best known ballad stanza is a quatrain consisting of alternating lines of iambic tetrameter and trimeter with end-rhymes on the short lines (abcb)—in the background possibly was the old Anglo-Saxon line, which if you will recall had three or four alliterated stresses. "Sir Patrick Spens" is as good an example as any:

The king sits in Dumferling town,
　　Drinking the blude-reid wine:
"O whar will I get guid sailor,
　　To sail this ship of mine?"

Up and spak an eldern knicht,
　　Sat at the king's richt knee:
"Sir Patrick Spens is the best sailor
　　That sails upon the sea."

The king has written a braid letter
　　And signed it wi' his hand,
And sent it to Sir Patrick Spens,
　　Was walking on the sand.

The first line that Sir Patrick read,
　　A loud lauch lauched he;
The next line that Sir Patrick read,
　　The tear blinded his ee.

"O wha is this has done this deed,
　　This ill deed done to me,
To send me out this time o' the year,
　　To sail upon the sea?

"Mak haste, mak haste, my mirry men all,
   Our guid ship sails the morn."
"O say na sae, my master dear,
   For I fear a deadly storm.

Late, late yestre'en I saw the new moon
   Wi' the auld moon in hir arm,
And I fear, I fear, my dear master,
   That we will come to harm."

O our Scots nobles were richt laith
   To weet their cork-heeled shoon,
But lang or a' the play were played
   Their hats they swam aboon.

O lang, lang may their ladies sit,
   Wi' their fans into their hand,
Or ere they see Sir Patrick Spens
   Come sailing to the land.

O lang, lang may the ladies stand
   Wi' their gold kems in their hair,
Waiting for their ain dear lords,
   For they'll see them na mair.

Half o'er, half o'er to Aberdour
   It's fifty fadom deep,
And there lies guid Sir Patrick Spens
   Wi' the Scots lords at his feet.

EXERCISE 6

Scan one or two stanzas of "Sir Patrick Spens" with respect to the beat just to get the feel of the ballad form. But do an extensive analysis of sound echoes, great and small, for the effect that they create.

In the light of what happens, the king's drinking of wine that is blood-red in the beginning assumes rather sinister implications, and blood-red then is not altogether as trite as one, perhaps, at first took it to be. But this aspect of "Sir Patrick Spens" requires more than passing notice. Time out for discussion . . .

The question is, do you want to work on a ballad now or later? Well, let's get started at least.

EXERCISE 7

Make up a sad story suitable for telling in ballad-form; if you wish, you can enter fully into the spirit of things by setting it in the Middle Ages, even narrating it in dialect. But that's not necessary; it can simply be about a lost dog or something like that. When you have the main outline of the story in your head, separate it into scenes and then portion the scenes into stanzas and begin writing.

Remember to keep to the basic pattern: four lines of alternating iambic tetrameter and trimeter with rhymes—like punctuation marks!—only on the short lines. Don't forget word and phrase repetition as well as that of the incremental variety at appropriate junctures.

In the eighteenth century a number of learned individuals began collecting and publishing the old ballads, among them Bishop Thomas Percy, whose *Reliques of Ancient English Poetry* (1765) in particular served as a kind of reader for the Romantic poets later in the century. The result was an imitation of the folk ballad, which we refer to today as the literary ballad, and the most notable effort in that direction was and still is "The Rime of the Ancient Mariner" by Samuel Taylor Coleridge (1772–1834).

The opening episode tells all:

It is an ancient Mariner,
And he stoppeth one of three.
"By thy long grey beard and glittering eye,
Now wherefore stopp'st thou me?

The Bridegroom's doors are opened wide,
And I am next of kin;
The guests are met, the feast is set:
May'st hear the merry din."

He holds him with his skinny hand,
"There was a ship," quoth he.
"Hold off! unhand me, grey-beard loon!"
Eftsoons his hand dropt he.

He holds him with his glittering eye—
The Wedding-Guest stood still,
And listens like a three years' child:
The Mariner hath his will.

The Wedding-Guest sat on a stone:
He cannot choose but hear;
And thus spake on that ancient man,
The bright-eyed Mariner.

"The ship was cheered, the harbour cleared,
Merrily did we drop
Below the kirk, below the hill,
Below the lighthouse top.

The Sun came up upon the left,
Out of the sea came he!
And he shone bright, and on the right
Went down into the sea.

Higher and higher every day,
Till over the mast at noon—"
The Wedding-Guest here beat his breast,
For he heard the loud bassoon.

The bride hath paced into the hall,
Red as a rose is she;
Nodding their heads before her goes
The merry minstrelsy.

The Wedding-Guest he beat his breast,
Yet he cannot choose but hear;
And thus spake on that ancient man,
The bright-eyed Mariner.

"And now the STORM-BLAST came, and he
Was tyrannous and strong:
He struck with his o'ertaking wings,
And chased us south along.

One of the problems that Coleridge had to face was possible boredom on the part of his readers, and one way that he relieved the monotony of the same form used for successive pages was occasionally to run the stanzas on. But generally he did not do this because self-containment of stanza was really a major feature of the old-time ballad, whose flavor he wanted to retain—it contributed to the overall terseness. So Coleridge used a poet's license, and here and there, where it seemed that the narrative would benefit from it, he inserted longer stanzas resembling the basic four-line one. For instance, the passage above in Part I is followed by:

With sloping masts and dipping prow,
As who pursued with yell and blow
Still treads the shadow of his foe,
And forward bends his head,
The ship drove fast, loud roared the blast,
And southward aye we fled.

But the rest of Part I is in the ballad stanza. In Part II the same strategy is employed, this time with two six-line stanzas following one another, both rhyming abcbdb. And then as of Part III Coleridge relaxed, and besides using that six-liner, he began inserting five-line stanzas rhyming abccb and aabcc, like this one:

We listened and looked sideways up!
Fear at my heart, as at a cup,
My life-blood seemed to sip!
The stars were dim, and thick the night,
The steersman's face by his lamp gleamed white.

Another six-line rhyming pattern emerges, abbbcb, and for the balance of the poem Coleridge continued to lace the ballad stanza with those four patterns. But of course the end of the "Rime" marks a return to the norm:

Farewell, farewell! but this I tell
To thee, thou Wedding-Guest!
He prayeth well, who loveth well
Both man and bird and beast.

He prayeth best, who loveth best
All things both great and small;
For the dear God who loveth us,
He made and loveth all.

The Mariner, whose eye is bright,
Whose beard with age is hoar,
Is gone: and now the Wedding-Guest
Turned from the bridegroom's door.

He went like one that hath been stunned,
And is of sense forlorn:
A sadder and a wiser man,
He rose the morrow morn.

Comparisons, as Mrs. Malaprop said, are odorous. Even so, here is what my student Joedy Lo Presto did in the form of a ballad:

WAKE UP AND SMELL THE COFFEE

When I was young, I dreamt the dreams
That young girls often fancy—
Of handsome princes on white steeds,
Of castles, balls, and dancing.

But later on, when my time came,
I didn't want to date.
For what real male could quite compare
With my ethereal mate?

Now many years have come and gone,
And still, I am alone.
They say that wisdom comes with age—
If so, I have not grown.

Oh where, oh where is my true love?
I'll send an SOS:
"Time's running out, so please respond—
"Help! Damsel in distress."

EXERCISE 8

If you have already begun on your ballad, consider spicing up the drama and cutting down on monotony with some stanzas of varying lengths. If you have no draft of a ballad yet, what else—get started!
And do what you will.

A POTPOURRI OF OTHER VERSE FORMS . . . NOT TO FORGET EXOTICA

Here are some other forms used by English poets of the past, including a few that are rather rare and unusual. If you are interested in a particular one or want to find it again in a hurry, they are given in order of stanza length, then rhythm, and finally bizarreness.

Terza rima

This was the stanza used by Dante (1265–1321) in his *Divine Comedy*, a poem of comparable length and complexity to *The Canterbury Tales*. Consisting of three lines with linking rhymes (aba, bcb, cdc, etc.), it works marvelously well in Italian because of the abundance of words with similar endings, but in English it's another story—as with the Petrarchan sonnet it's devilishly difficult. Clearly the prize goes to Percy Bysshe Shelley (1792–1822) for his handling of terza rima in his "Ode to the West Wind." Addressing the Wind, as he has been doing all along, the "I" concludes:

> Make me thy lyre, even as the forest is:
> What if my leaves are falling like its own!
> The tumult of thy mighty harmonies
>
> Will take from both a deep, autumnal tone,
> Sweet though in sadness. Be thou, Spirit fierce,
> My spirit! Be thou me, impetuous one!
>
> Drive my dead thoughts over the universe
> Like withered leaves to quicken a new birth!
> And, by the incantation of this verse,
>
> Scatter, as from an unextinguished hearth
> Ashes and sparks, my words among mankind!
> Be through my lips to unawakened earth
>
> The trumpet of a prophecy! O, Wind,
> If Winter comes, can Spring be far behind?

Note the final couplet—this was Shelley's touch, not Dante's.

EXERCISE 9

See what you can do with terza rima—let's say, a poem of three stanzas, and of course, partial rhymes are fine. If you wish to parody Shelley—many people in the past would have liked to—don't be shy. The same goes for sending him an answer from the Wind.

The In Memoriam *quatrain*

There are quatrains and quatrains. We have already covered two—the elegiac, consisting of cross-rhymed iambic pentameter lines, and the ballad stanza, alternating iambic tetrameter and trimeter with rhymes on the short lines—and taken passing notice of another in Wordsworth's "A Slumber Did My Spirit Seal," where he used straight iambic tetrameter with cross-rhymes. Following in Wordsworth's footsteps, Tennyson adopted a four-line iambic tetrameter stanza for his major work, *In Memoriam* (1850), in which he mourned the death of a close college friend. But instead of cross-rhymes, he employed an envelope rhyme (abba), reminiscent of the octave of the Petrarchan sonnet.

Consider the beginning:

> I held it truth, with him who sings
>   To one clear harp in divers tones,
>   That men may rise on stepping-stones
> Of their dead selves to higher things.
>
> But who shall so forecast the years
>   And find in loss a gain to match?
>   Or reach a hand through time to catch
> The far-off interest of tears?
>
> Let Love clasp Grief lest both be drowned,
>   Let darkness keep her raven gloss.
>   Ah, sweeter to be drunk with loss,
> To dance with Death, to beat the ground,
>
> Than that the victor Hours should scorn
>   The long result of love, and boast,
>   "Behold the man that loved and lost,
> But all he was is overworn."

Clearly what we have here, whether intended or not, is a couplet within another couplet, and the result is that the third line receives extra emphasis because of the immediate repetition of the second rhyme. Note how Tennyson achieved variation and avoided monotony by running on some of the stanzas.

EXERCISE 10

Try composing a poem of your own of three or so *In Memoriam* quatrains.

Rime royale and ottava rima

Chaucer used the rime royale stanza, consisting of seven lines and obviously of French origin, for his other long poem, *Troilus and Criseyde*, a story of love and intrigue. He began it:

The double sorwe of Troilus to tellen,	*sorrow*
That was the kyng Priamus sone of Troye,	
In lovynge, how his aventures fellen	
Fro wo to wele, and after out of joie,	
My purpos is, er that I parte fro ye.	
Thesiphone, thow help me for t'endite	*indite*
Thise woful vers, that wepen as I write.	*weep*

As one can see, the rhyme scheme is ababbcc, and typically the final couplet is set off from the rest of the stanza. Variation was achieved by running on the final couplet with the first five lines and, more often, by making a syntactic unit of the fifth line and the final couplet.

Bearing a close affinity to rime royale in terms of strategy is the eight-line ottava rima stanza, the medium of the fourteenth-century Italian poets Ariosto and Tasso, which Byron used with such success in his long satiric epic *Don Juan*. Consisting of an alternately rhyming sestet followed by a couplet (abababcc), it proved more manageable than rime royale, allowing for a balanced narrative punctuated by a witty comment in the single couplet at the end, which had a snap to it.

Here again is one of *Don Juan*'s crescendos:

'T is pity learnéd virgins ever wed
   With persons of no sort of education,
Or gentlemen, who, though well born and bred,
   Grow tired of scientific conversation:
I don't choose to say much upon this head,
   I'm a plain man, and in a single station,
But—Oh! ye lords of ladies intellectual,
Inform us truly, have they not hen-pecked you all?

Clearly anything goes—and did go—with the rhyme.

EXERCISE 11

   If you've already attempted an imitation of ottava rima in Chapter Five with respect to polysyllabic rhyme, dig it out and work on it some more—MORE! If not, try and write one now, and remember—for that true Byronic flavor, the crazier and more complicated the rhymes the better. Just so long as you have eight lines of iambic pentameter rhyming abababcc.

The Spenserian

What book on traditional English verse would be complete without a reference to Sir Edmund Spenser (1552–99), author of *The Faerie Queene*, a long intricate political and theological allegory in which Elizabeth I was glorified, along with virtue as the people of that time understood it. For this work Spenser devised a stanza of his own, consisting of eight lines of iambic pentameter followed by an alexandrine (iambic hexameter) with a rhyme scheme of ababbcbcc, as follows:

> Redoubted knights, and honorable Dames,
>   To whom I levell all my labours end,
>   Right sore I feare, least with unworthy blames   *lest*
>   This odious argument my rimes should shend,   *shame*
>   Or ought your goodly patience offend,
>   Whiles of a wanton Lady I do write,
>   Which with her loose incontinence doth blend   *blind*
>   The shyning glory of your soveraigne light,
> And knighthood fowle defacéd by a faithlesse knight.

A great favorite of the Romantic poets, Spenserian stanzas were used successively by Wordsworth, Shelley, and Byron, but truly the masterpiece is Keats' "The Eve of St. Agnes," in which the poet retold the story of Romeo and Juliet with a happy ending—that is, if you can call the pair of young lovers running away together in a terrible gale happy:

> And they are gone: ay, ages long ago
> These lovers fled away into the storm.
> That night the Baron dreamt of many a woe,
> And all his warrior-guests, with shade and form
> Of witch, and demon, and large coffin-worm,
> Were long be-nightmar'd. Angela the old
> Died palsy-twitch'd, with meagre face deform;
> The Beadsman, after thousand aves told,
> For aye unsought for slept among his ashes cold.

Note here (as well as in Spenser's original above) how the "b" rhyme ("storm"/"form"/"coffin-worm"/"deform") dominates the stanza until it intermingles with the "c" rhyme ("old") and becomes lost in the end-line echoes of the couplet ("told"/"cold").

EXERCISE 12

Write a poem in one or more Spenserian stanzas. If you wish, set it vaguely in the Middle Ages, as Keats did in his in imitation of the master, Spenser.

Anapestic and trochaic verse

As we have said, traditional English poetry written exclusively in anapests or trochees is few and far between compared to that in iambs. Still, there are several notable examples in each, among them, if you

like that sort of thing, "The Night Before Christmas" ("'Twas the
night before Christmas and all through the house") by Clement Moore
and Longfellow's "Hiawatha" ("By the shores of Gichee-goomee").

More to my taste, and, I hope, yours, are the ventures in anapests
and trochees of William Blake (1757–1827). Look, for instance, at the
languorously sad tone that he was able to sustain throughout "Nurse's
Song" in *Songs of Innocence* by means of the anapest's long foot:

When the voices of children are heard on the green
And laughing is heard on the hill,
My heart is at rest within my breast
  And everything else is still.

"Then come home, my children, the sun is gone down
"And the dews of night arise;
"Come, come, leave off play, and let us away
"Till the morning appears in the skies.

"No, no, let us play, for it is yet day
"And we cannot go to sleep;
"Besides, in the sky the little birds fly
"And the hills are all cover'd with sheep.

"Well, well, go & play till the light fades away
"And then go home to bed.
The little ones leaped & shouted & laugh'd
  And all the hills ecchoed.

But a poem in pure anapests it is not, nor should it be.

EXERCISE 13

Do a scansion of "Nurse's Song" in order to see this, and note at the
same time the end-rhymes on the second and fourth lines. What stan-
zaic form that we have covered does this remind you of?

EXERCISE 14

Try a three-stanza poem in anapests yourself, remembering that, like
it or not, there are going to be substitutions galore. Try for a pastoral or
rural setting like Blake's if you wish.

"The Tyger" from Blake's *Songs of Experience* is obviously a masterpiece of trochaic verse:

Tyger! Tyger! burning bright
In the forests of the night,
What immortal hand or eye
Could frame thy fearful symmetry?

In what distant deeps or skies
Burnt the fire of thine eyes?
On what wings dare he aspire?
What the hand dare seize the fire?

And what shoulder, & what art,
Could twist the sinews of thy heart?
And when thy heart began to beat,
What dread hand? & what dread feet?

What the hammer? What the chain?
In what furnace was thy brain?
What the anvil? What dread grasp
Dare its deadly terrors clasp?

When the stars threw down their spears,
And water'd heaven with their tears,
Did he smile his work to see?
Did he who made the Lamb make thee?

Tyger! Tyger! burning bright
In the forests of the night,
What immortal hand or eye
Dare frame thy fearful symmetry?

But even after a cursory glance, it turns out that trochees are as difficult to sustain as anapests. Consider "And water'd heaven with their tears," for instance. Is it or isn't it iambic?

EXERCISE 15

Now give "The Tyger" a careful going over from start to finish.

EXERCISE 16

Try a trochaic poem in three stanzas yourself now, again with it clearly understood that there will be considerable infiltration by iambs. Try to make it about something of natural force and power like a tiger.

Exotica

Here are a group of French imports, much beloved by the English Victorians, that are simply fun to know—*ballade, rondeau, roundel, triolet,* and *villanelle.* All depending for their effect on refrains as well as involved rhyme schemes, they invite comparison with embroidery in their intricacy.

The *ballade* consists of three octets rhyming ababbcbc, followed by an envoi (a final stanza serving as a summary or dedication) in the form of a cross-rhyming quatrain; the last line of each stanza including the latter is the same. The most famous *ballade* ever penned is "The Ballade of Dead Ladies" by François Villon (ca. 1431–63). Here is Dante Gabriel Rossetti's masterly translation:

Tell me now in what hidden way is
   Lady Flora the lovely Roman?
Where's Hipparchia, and where is Thaïs,
    Neither of them the fairer woman?
    Where is Echo, beheld of no man,
Only heard on river and mere—
    She whose beauty was more than human? . . .
But where are the snows of yester-year?

Where's Héloïse, the learned nun,
   For whose sake Abeillard, I ween,
Lost manhood and put priesthood on?
    (From Love he won such dule and teen)
    And where, I pray you, is the Queen
Who willed that Buridan should steer
    Sewed in a sack's mouth down the Seine? . . .
But where are the snows of yester-year?

White Queen Blanche, like a queen of lilies,
   With a voice like any mermaiden—
Bertha Broadfoot, Beatrice, Alice,
    And Ermengarde the Lady of Maine—
    And that good Joan whom Englishmen
At Rouen doomed and burned her there—
    Mother of God, where are they, then? . . .
But where are the snows of yester-year?

                  Envoy
Nay, never ask this week, fair lord,
   Where they are gone, nor yet this year,
Except with this for an overword—
But where are the snows of yester-year?

There have been a number of varieties of *rondeau*; the modern version, as found, for instance, in "A Rondeau to Ethel" by Austin Dobson (1840–1921) consists of three stanzas of five, three, and five lines employing the same two rhymes throughout, with a refrain at the beginning of the first stanza and at the end of each of the others:

"In teacup-times"! The style of dress
Would suit your beauty, I confess;
   BELINDA-like, the patch you'd wear;

I picture you with powdered hair,—
You'd make a charming Shepherdess!

And I—no doubt—could well express
Sir PLUME'S complete conceitedness,—
    Could poise a clouded cane with care
            "In teacup-times"!

The parts would fit precisely—yes:
We should achieve a huge success!
    You should disdain, and I despair,
    With quite the true Augustan air;
But . . . could I love you more, or less—
            "In teacup-times"?

The *roundel* as rendered by Algernon Charles Swinburne (1837–1909) has a similar structure but with fewer lines:

A Roundel is wrought as a ring or a starbright sphere,
With craft of delight and with cunning of sound unsought,
That the heart of the hearer may smile if to pleasure his ear
        A roundel is wrought.

Its jewel of music is carven of all or of aught—
Love, laughter, or mourning—remembrance or rapture or fear—
That fancy may fashion to hang in the ear of thought.

As a bird's quick song runs round, and the hearts in us hear—
Pause answers to pause, and again the same strain caught,
So moves the device whence, round as a pearl or tear,
        A roundel is wrought.

Note the use of round objects—ring, sphere, pearl, tear, etc.—as well as the many "r"'s to suggest "rounding."

Two other related forms—the *rondeau redoublé* and *rondel* [sic]—we pass over in silence.

Eight lines rhyming abaaabab and two refrains are employed in the *triolet*; one of the refrains is repeated three times, hence the name of this form. Consider "Kiss" by Austin Dobson:

Rose kissed me today,
    Will she kiss me tomorrow?
Let it be as it may,
Rose kissed me today.
But the pleasure gives way
    To a savor of sorrow;—

Rose kissed me today,—
Will she kiss me tomorrow?

In the *villanelle* two rhymes and two refrains are employed in five ter-
cets and a quatrain as follows, in Dobson's "For a Copy of Theocritus":

O SINGER of the field and fold,
Theocritus! Pan's pipe was thine,—
Thine was the happier Age of Gold.

For thee the scent of new-turned mould,
The bee-hives, and the murmuring pine.
O Singer of the field and fold!

Thou sang'st the simple feasts of old,—
The beechen bowl made glad with wine . . .
Thine was the happier Age of Gold.

Thou bad'st the rustic loves be told,—
Thou bad'st the tuneful reeds combine,
O Singer of the field and fold!

And round thee, ever-laughing, rolled
The blithe and blue Sicilian brine . . .
Thine was the happier Age of Gold.

Alas for us! Our songs are cold;
Our Northern suns too sadly shine:—
O Singer of the field and fold,
Thine was the happier Age of Gold!

EXERCISE 17

You should at least take a stab at one refrain poem. If you are particularly adept at rhyme, go for the *villanelle*; if not, try whatever seems
the easiest to handle—or better yet, make up your own variant. Just be
sure to use a refrain or refrains and a limited number of rhymes—like
two. And oh yes, feel free to be as silly as you please. And of course give
your new form a name.

Before you dismiss the above pieces of exotica as being utterly inane,
take a look some time at Dylan Thomas' masterly *villanelle*, "Do Not Go
Gentle into That Good Night," where that line and "Rage, rage against
the dying of the light" are powerfully interwoven.

CHAPTER EIGHT
Free verse—it isn't for free

Welcome back, time traveler. Having touched on various parts of our poetic past, like so many butterflies flitting from petal to petal, we are now ready to move on to the anti-past—or back to the free verse antipasto, if you will.

As I said, free verse, which has laws unto itself with no set rhythm or meter or sound pattern, came as a reaction to tradition. Poets began writing in free verse in the latter part of the nineteenth century in opposition to the rules of traditional English verse, which they felt were restraints on their feelings and ability to express themselves.

But there was, still is and forevermore will be one great drawback to writing free verse—each free verse poem has its own rhythm and sound correspondences, which have been chosen by the poet alone with reference only to his or her sensibility. And this—following the dictates of one's own self, one's own ear—can turn out to be a form of tyranny far worse than being subjected to a bunch of outside rules and regulations. Consider—with the latter you either succeed or don't succeed, whereas one's own standards may be difficult or even impossible to attain, and one may flounder, go from pillar to post in search of the right effect and perhaps never quite find it. So a word to the wise—having arrived at free verse in this book, don't think that you're home free!

The question may arise—if free verse can be in whatever rhythm or rhythms a poet feels like using, with any sequence of sounds, what makes it poetry as distinguished from prose? The answer is simply degree—any group of intelligible words has rhythm and sound echoes of a sort; free verse generally has them to a greater degree or with more deliberateness than prose.

There is of course an area in which the two overlap—the prose poem, in which for reasons best known to a poet, he or she chose to set forth a poem in sentences and paragraphs; and lyrical prose, where a novelist or story writer elected to make readers feel along with him or her in poetical terms. As an example of a successful prose poem, take a look some time at James Agee's *Knoxville Summer: 1915*; as for lyrical writers of prose, there are any number of them, including Herman Melville in his *Moby Dick*, already cited. Not to be confused with these is poetry that is prosaic, meaning flat and uninteresting, and prose that is heavily laden with inappropriate ornaments, labeled by some florid or flowery.

One of the advantages of writing in free verse is that a wide variety of effects is possible owing to that same broad liberty to pick and choose among rhythms and sounds that I have been warning about. For instance, look at the texture of these few lines of Allen Ginsberg's "Howl":

> I saw the best minds of my generation destroyed by madness, starving,
>   hysterical naked,
> dragging themselves through the negro streets at dawn looking for an
>   angry fix,
> angelheaded hipsters burning for the ancient heavenly connection to the
>   starry dynamo in the machinery of night,
> who poverty and tatters and hollow-eyed and high sat up smoking in the
>   supernatural darkness of cold-water flats floating across the tops of
>   cities contemplating jazz,
> who bared their brains to Heaven under the El and saw Mohammedan
>   angels staggering on tenement roofs illuminated, . . .

And compare them with the following snippet from Sylvia Plath's "Cut":

> What a thrill—
> My thumb instead of an onion.
> The top quite gone
> Except for a sort of a hinge
>
> Of skin,
> A flap like a hat,
> Dead white.
> Then that red plush.
>
> Little pilgrim,
> The Indian's axed your scalp.
> Your turkey wattle
> Carpet rolls
>
> Straight from the heart.
> I step on it,
> Clutching my bottle
> Of pink fizz . . .

I certainly seem to have exaggerated matters by citing these two poems that are so very different. But no, I don't believe so; truly in the end, every good free verse poem should add a leaf to exaggeration where free verse is concerned—should be distinctive in some way, in other words.

Two major technical considerations are involved in composing poems in free verse. Actually we have encountered them before, but now we are going to do so from the point of view of free verse alone—they are how you arrange your words on lines and what sounds you use.

LINE ARRANGEMENT: IT'S SIMPLY A MATTER OF LOGIC

Since literally anything goes in free verse, lines can be arranged however one wishes and can be of any length. The only consideration is that the arrangement feel "right" to the poet—though, of course, inevitably it becomes a matter of whether readers in-the-know agree.

How do you know when something is "right"? Simply by working at it and working at it until you get a sense that something is settled; less desirable but acceptable obviously is a point when you feel that what you've ended up with is the best solution under the circumstances—it's almost "right" but not quite. Working at it may mean creating stanzas, re-arranging lines, transferring one or more words from one line to another—and maybe even, after endless shuffling around, coming back to the arrangement that one originally had!

Let's consider William Carlos Williams' celebrated poem "The Red Wheelbarrow." Please understand, I'm not for the moment suggesting that Williams went through any of what I have just been describing—rather, I would like for us to explore his idea of "rightness" by looking at his other options.

"The Red Wheelbarrow" is a very simple poem, really a single sentence broken up into four stanzas of two lines each, the first of which in each instance consists of three or four syllables, the second of two:

so much depends
upon

a red wheel
barrow

glazed with rain
water

beside the white
chickens.

Now note what happens when we write it out as a single sentence:

So much depends upon a red wheel barrow glazed with rain water
beside the white chickens.

It doesn't seem to say very much, does it? In fact, one's reaction is
likely to be, "So what."
Let's try it as a single stanza—

so much depends
upon
a red wheel
barrow
glazed with rain
water
beside the white
chickens.

Something is lacking here as well—those long pauses that the separate
stanzas betoken are necessary, it seems.
Getting rid of all those short lines doesn't do the trick either—

so much depends upon
a red wheel barrow
glazed with rain water
beside the white chickens.

On the other hand, are all four of those stanzas necessary? Let's see—

so much depends
upon
a red wheel
barrow

glazed with rain
water
beside the white
chickens.

That seems better, but there's an awkward split between the barrow
and its glaze. So how about—

so much depends
upon

a red wheel
barrow
glazed with rain
water
beside the white
chickens.

or—

so much depends
upon

a red wheel
barrow
glazed with rain
water

beside the white
chickens.

Neither is quite IT because now too much of the burden falls on the
barrow and its glaze. Four stanzas seem to be the answer then, but what
about the arrangement of words within each of them? Here are three
possibilities:

so much
depends upon

a red
wheel barrow

glazed with
rain water
beside the
white chickens.

*

so
much depends upon

a
red wheel barrow

glazed
with rain water

beside
the white chickens.

*

so much depends
upon

a red
wheel barrow

glazed
with rain water

beside the
white chickens.

Dizzying, isn't it? And sobering, I hope.

So what makes Williams' particular arrangement a success? Focus is the answer. And that focus cannot be too long anymore than it can be too short; this will not do either—

So
much
depends
upon

a
red
wheel
barrow

glazed
with
rain
water

beside
the
white
chickens.

No, it must be just so, with the first stanza introducing—

so much depends
upon

and those that follow each presenting a picture, a very precise picture, which it is necessary to see part by part—

a red wheel
barrow

glazed with rain
water

beside the white
chickens.

Concomitant with this scene that Williams was inviting us to behold as he beheld it is the rhythm or cadence that results from the shorter line following the longer line—which seems to underline Williams' vision, as if he were saying, "Look—LOOK!"

EXERCISE 1

Get hold of the whole of Sylvia Plath's "Cut" and try arranging it differently as I did above, first as to stanza and then individual line. Don't be lazy, do a thorough job. It's important that you see what happens for yourself.

If a copy of this poem does not come readily to hand, choose another from an anthology of contemporary poetry; a relatively brief one is obviously more easily managed.

P.S. What do you suppose would be the result if you tried rearranging the selection from Ginsberg's "Howl"? Mind you, I'm not recommending that you do anything of the sort. Just think about it.

Sometimes it happens that someone comes up with an arrangement that seems better than the poet's. This requires discussion, no? So do discuss. The poet may have thought of it too, and rejected it for some reason. What could that reason have been?

EXERCISE 2

Here's something different—anything goes. Take the following, which is *not* a poem, and try three or four different stanza and line arrangements as if it were:

She sits with tears on her cheek, her chin on her hand,
the child in her lap, his nose pressed to the glass.

What different effects does each arrangement give you? Which one do you prefer? Why?

EXERCISE 3

Take some short poem of your own and try rearranging it as we have above. If you don't want to do this—some students feel that it's desecrating—or you don't have a suitable guinea pig, extract a piece of prose from a newspaper or textbook, or even this book, and practice different stanza and line arrangements.

This brings up a rather delicate subject. What is to stop you from calling the result of your newspaper or textbook exercise a poem? To tell the truth, nothing. Anything is a poem that you care to make into one. Of course, whether or not it is enjoyable and of interest to other people is another story.

Finally, before we turn to the matter of sound proper, one should be aware that sound enters into how lines and stanzas are arranged, in that each break, whether mid- or end-line or stanza, brings with it a silence, and in free verse silences can be as much a part of sound as utterances themselves. One can even speak of qualities of silence, depending on what has come before and after. It's something like negative space (the space around) in sculpture.

When one reads "The Red Wheelbarrow" as written, it becomes necessary to pause slightly in the middle of each long line—after "much," "red," "glazed," and "beside"—and longer at the end of each line. The result is a kind of fine tuning of the separate images, as if we were giving a last little turn to a pair of binoculars or a camera lens. The silence after "rain" is particularly effective, allowing us to see the wheel barrow "glazed with rain" and "glazed with rain water," as if through a bubble.

IT HAS TO SOUND "RIGHT" TOO

The rule of thumb concerning actual echoes in free verse is the same as that with line and stanza arrangement—the sounds should correspond with and in some cases enhance what you are trying to convey, and should help establish a mood or contribute to a tone. Other than that, the poet is free to use pure as well as partial rhyme if it suits his or her purposes.

One danger of using sounds freely is to get so carried away as to lose sight of sense. To do this would be tantamount to creating word salad, and even as a form of rebellion, it won't do—it's been done too many times already and by now it's just plain boring.

Let's take another look at Williams' "The Red Wheelbarrow," now for its sounds:

so much depends
upon

a red wheel
barrow

glazed with rain
water

beside the white
chickens.

No question about it, the echoes that Williams chose serve to support the peacefulness of the scene. Soft sounds like "n"'s, "l"'s, "r"'s, and "s"'s predominate—they mute the few hard sounds, like the "d"'s in "depend," "glazed," and "beside." Some unobtrusive assonance serves to link within stanzas: the "uh" in "much" and "upon," the "a" in "glazed" and "rain," and the "ai" in "beside" and "white."

All in all, one is bound to conclude that there's nothing much here, and that's just the point. Just like the number of syllables and words per line, and the very number of stanzas, all the sound echoes in "The Red Wheelbarrow" come in small handfuls.

Was it an accident that the echoes came out so effectively in support of the sense? Not at all. Williams chose them carefully, that is, he selected the words with care as to both sense and sound. And there's something else that has come to separate free verse from traditional poetry. Where the latter was rhymed, one was on the lookout for words with similar sounds that would somehow make do where sense was concerned; with free verse, unless one is writing a loose hit-or-miss kind of thing like Ginsberg, the important thing is the right word with its sound. To see what I mean, try substituting a synonym for "glazed" in "The Red Wheelbarrow"—try, oh say, "shiny," "gleaming," or "slicked" for starters. See what I mean?

EXERCISE 4

Take the poem that you used for line and stanza arrangement in Exercise 1 and examine the sound correspondences in it—try changing them by substituting synonyms.

Quite possibly as with the line and stanza arrangements, someone will come up with a word that seems to work better in its place than the poet's choice. What's the story? Discuss, discuss.

EXERCISE 5

Dig out the arrangement that you made of:

She sits with tears on her cheek, her chin on her hand, the child in her lap, his nose pressed to the glass.

See if you can do anything with the sounds, either to make the passage sound "better" or to enhance its meaning.

Remember above all, when you are reading these "exercise poems" aloud or comparing notes with someone, that there is no one answer as there is in math. As many as half a dozen people may come up with quite different results that are all striking in their way.

Psst! Are you one of them?

EXERCISE 6

Take in hand that poem of your own or extract of prose you worked on in Exercise 3 and zero in on the sounds.

One important thing to bear in mind—never forget it with regard to anything that you write—is that deciding on no change after a thorough review is perfectly all right.

EXERCISE 7

If you have already written poems in free verse, now is a good time to find them and examine them both as to line and stanza arrangement and sound echoes. If you have never written anything in free verse, it's time now to spread your poetical wings and try something of your own in your own way.

When you are finished, exchange with a classmate or friend. No question about it—you'll both be kind, won't you?

If you live in the middle of a wasteland and there is no one to commune with—but absolutely no one—send it to me.

I just ask this. One poem, pleeze!

CHAPTER NINE
Getting started—again

"Our revels all are ended"—who said that? Unless you strongly insist on its being otherwise, it's time now to put away the exercises that you did in the preceding chapters, including the grades that you received on them if you were in a class, and strike out on your own.

Why am I so confident in you, so sure that you are a poet? Because by enrolling in a poetry workshop and sticking with it or acquiring this book and going it on your own, you have so defined yourself—you are a poet. What kind of and how successful a poet remains to be seen.

THE BLANK PAGE SYNDROME

Sometimes when a student—or should I say a former student—has reached this point of being encouraged to do anything that he or she wants, panic sets in. The person takes pen in hand, and nothing comes—but nothing. Well, take it from me, there's no worse form of self-torture than to force oneself to sit and stare at a blank page.

What should you do then? By all means get away from that dreadful white shadow—sometimes for symbolic reasons it proves beneficial to crumple it up and throw it in the waste basket. Go and sit or lie down somewhere else, where it is quiet of course, or go for a stroll—remember, poets stroll. Reading is another possibility, the works of poets both of the past and present, as well as those of the great writers of lyrical prose. In other words, follow the suggestions given in Chapter Two for finding your own personal style or idiom. In fact, if you haven't done that yet, now is the time to address yourself to that issue. Turn back to Chapter Two to see where you left off.

Other possibilities will present themselves—like having something to eat or drink. Everyone has his or her own "poison." Returning to the place where you normally do your writing after a while and just scribbling or listing words and phrases as we did in Chapter One sometimes does the trick.

While many poets prefer to be alone and, indeed, make very poor spouses, requiring a special kind of mate capable of weathering periods of being ignored, the problem with you may be that you are naturally gregarious and this kind of isolation doesn't appeal to you. In that case there is only one solution—find some company, either a kindred spirit, even if it is through the mail, or a group. If you can't locate a group in your neck of the woods—usually your local librarian can be very helpful—form one of your own! As a last resort, there is always a poetry workshop if you've never taken one, or another if you have—but only for the sake of communing. Don't go making the mistake of remaining a student of poetry writing—of telling yourself and everyone else that you're going to be or are (ugh!) studying to be a poet. Remember, you are—you have arrived!

However you manage it, once launched on your first poem, you usually don't stop, but go on and on, turning out one after another, sometimes in a rush, sometimes haltingly. There are dry periods, of course. But not to worry, the spark or whatever it is generally comes back.

Contemporary poets Ruth Fainlight and Colette Inez both very gladly obliged when I asked them to share with us how they began individual works. Ruth Fainlight chose as her subject her poem "The Prism":

> Braided like those plaits of multi-
> coloured threads my mother kept
> in her workbox (beige, flesh, and fawn
> for mending stockings, primary tones
> to match our playclothes, grey and black
> for Daddy's business suits), or Medusa-
> coils of telephone wires, vivid
> as internal organs exposed in their packed
> logic under the pavement, nestling
> in the gritty London clay,
> associations fray into messages:
>
> codes to unravel, cords to follow
> out of prison, poems which make
> no concession, but magnify
> the truth of every note and colour,
> indifferent whether they blind or deafen
> or ravish or are ignored; the blueprint
> of a shelter against the glare
> —and the waterfall to build it near—
> the perfect place to sit and hear
> that choir of hymning voices, and watch
> the prism of the rainbow spray.

Concerning this poem she explains:

"I must have been reading something about prisms, because my first draft of this poem begins:

Like a prism which captures and divides
white light into all the rainbow's colours,
the focus of a poem can expand
one strand of thought into its hundred
sources, memories, and images.

—which sounds like a note to myself about the poem's subject, rather than poetry—or like a motor running itself in. Quite often, I've noticed, the first lines one writes serve that purpose.

"On the same sheet of paper there are more lines, specific images now:

Braided like falling water . . .

(which introduces the idea of a waterfall, though in the finished poem it appears many lines later) and continuing:

                    . . . or those
plaits of different coloured threads
my mother kept in her workbox.

"With the words 'braided' and 'plait' I had arrived at the core image. 'Coils,' 'wires,' 'fray,' 'unravel,' and 'cords' follow this thread, and lead to the waterfall, which I visualised as a many-stranded white curtain, like the white light which a prism splits into the colours of the rainbow.

"It took several more drafts, though, before I discarded that first too-abstract statement. Until then, as if unconsciously aware that it had quite a different character, I felt forced to isolate it, and tried to fit everything into a structure of five-lined stanzas. The moment I allowed my mother's sewing-thread to lead me further into the labyrinth, it became apparent where each line should end, and the rest of what I had written separated naturally into two eleven-lined stanzas.

"Telephone wires brought sound as well as sight into the poem—messages and codes and voices. Light waves were equated to sound waves as I worked to express my intuition that the plaited threads, the coiled telephone wires under the pavement, the vivid organs inside our bodies, and the rainbow in the spray were visual equivalents to the endless richness of verbal associations. Poems made from words can ravish with their beauty, blind or deafen with their spectrums of sound and colour and, even if ignored, still serve as shelters and the blueprints for them.

"I try to keep the words of a poem close to the feelings and sensations that inspired it, in the hope that it will inspire the same feelings, recognitions, and memories in its reader. In this way, he or she becomes involved in its reality, even a participant in its creation—because reading is an active relationship between reader and writer.

"But writing is a relationship between writer and language. A poem develops organically from the first inspiring phrase. That phrase, or cluster of words, includes every essential element, and it is of the utmost importance to allow all its potential of sound and meaning to realise themselves. At times, when I am working on a poem, it can develop in unexpected ways.

"I re-read what had been written during the course of several days, on many sheets of paper. I had not known where the poem would lead me when I began it. There was no choir of hymning voices until the shelter near the waterfall came into being and I, and whoever else might read the poem, could sit inside and hear that song of praise—and 'watch the prism of the rainbow spray.'

"Explanation and paraphrasing have become direct quotation. There is no other way to say what a poem tries to say than by the exact order of the words of that very poem.

Colette Inez's experience with her poem "Apothegms and Counsels" was of another order:

Scratch a poet and you'll find affinities. One may be set off by a good bottle of Bordeaux, another by aardvarks or some other eccentricity. I'm hooked on Holiday Inns, or rather on their dining rooms. While the chain's motel rooms seem cloned—to hold down a sense of dislocation among traveling salesmen, I'm told—almost anything goes for theme settings in their restaurants. Instance: Cleveland's Holiday Inn features a revival of World War I air wars in its Red Baron Room.

A diorama of von Richtofen's aerial exploits. Checkerboard Fokkers decimating Allied Spads and Neuports. Smoking coffins for our young lads, spiraling by the score to violent ends as the Red Baron notches yet another Yank in his gunsights.

Bizarre. But there's something to be made of this inspired masochism. Carry it one step forward and we have:

A Wehrmacht chain of restaurants,
our former enemies as kitsch,
example: Hitler House, The Goebbels Room,
Eva Braun Chalet, souvenir whips and swastikas
in multicolored marzipan

I jotted this in my journal in a room whose ceilings and walls were lanced with incandescent tracers scoring bull's-eyes behind diners' tables. Amazement gave way to a leap of memory: a friend who found 'Love' at the signature of a stranger's letter wholly improper. I disagreed in a passage I attached to another budding poem:

I never find love at the close of a letter
offensive.
Very truly yours bends my ear.
Very truly yours wants my bankbook
and remittance.
Very truly yours writes the world.

What had I done? Coined a few axioms, but why stop there? The poem *could* evolve with a handful of other minor homilies for these times. Four, in all, wrote themselves on the facing journal page, a first draft of 'Apothegms and Counsels,' a reflection on relative weights and sizes:

If someone says you're too short,
say diamond rings don't come in cartons.

If someone says you're too large,
say you're an Amazon at large.

If someone says your breasts are too big,
say you bought them in Katmandu
and the fitting rooms were dark.

If someone says your breasts are too small,
say chickpeas are loved in Prague.

How much do I weigh on the sun? On the moon?

I weigh two tons on the sun.
I weigh twenty pounds on the moon.
Love makes me weightless.

It soon dawned on me that Teutonic asides and correspondence closings seemed beside the point. So I abandoned them, allowing the second draft of my poem to indulge only in figures of speech for its content. Cutting it back to the purity of counsels, I also took out the clutter of numerical values; 'tons' on the sun and 'pounds' on the moon could stand alone. I shifted to an imaginary, feisty and commanding *you* to give the poem universality. And, in a final resolution, the last quatrain was burnished several months later.

APOTHEGMS AND COUNSELS

If someone says you're too short,
say diamond pins don't come in cartons.

If someone says you're too large,
say you're an Amazon at large.

If someone says your breasts are too big,
say you bought them in Katmandu

and the fitting rooms were dark.

Say chickpeas are loved in Prague
if someone says your breasts are too small.

How much do you weigh on the sun? On the moon?

Tons on the sun.
Less on the moon.
Love makes you weightless.

If someone says you're far too out,
say Doppler Effect,
that you're writing a history of light
for the children of Pythagoras.

WHITHER WILLST, WIT

Now let's say that you take to this business of being a poet, and are writing regularly, what then? Well, everything begins with the end of *Paradise Lost*—as a poet, the world is all before you.

First and foremost, you will want to try to get some of your work in print for others to read besides your friends. By this I mean in literary magazines, and an exhaustive list of same can be found in the *Directory of Poetry Publishers*, available in the reference section of public libraries. If you're planning on a long campaign, you might want to invest in your own copy by writing to the publisher: Dustbooks, Box 100, Paradise, CA 95969. Your object will be to find some magazines that might be receptive to your work, in other words that publish poems in a style similar to yours or echoing some of your sentiments or pet concerns. Pinpointing the right magazines among such a multitude is no easy job—you'll have to go through the directory page by page, make a list of possibilities, and then either begin sending out blindly or try to obtain a copy of each of the magazines and examine them yourself. But warning: most libraries and bookstores carry very few literary magazines, so don't count on finding the ones that you want to look at in yours, and you are going to have to be patient if you order them through inter-library loan or send for them directly from the publishers.

So you have a list of magazines that might be attracted to your work, what do you do then? Choose three poems and write a cover letter, telling them what is enclosed, that you are familiar with some of the poetry in their magazine and think that yours would be of interest to their readership too, and then identify yourself as a poet in some way—that you have been writing for so long, etc. Don't hesitate to advise that if they accept, this would be your first publication. Many editors of small magazines pride themselves on discovering new talent. Be sure that you enclose an SASE (self-addressed stamped envelope)—and, above all, that you have not parted with your only copies of the poems!

Some magazines frown on multiple submissions, others encourage it, still others don't care. Read the entry in the Dustbook directory carefully and be advised accordingly. If you do submit a poem to several places at the same time, keep a careful record, and if and when you receive an acceptance, notify the other magazines of it at once as a matter of courtesy, so they won't waste time reading and considering something that they will not be able to use.

As soon as you've sent off your poems, get busy on something else; if you can't write, do busy work, clean out drawers, closets, etc. Whatever you do, don't by any means live to check out the mail every day because you may have a long wait. The waiting period for work submitted is spelled out in the Dustbook directory, and varies from several weeks to months. If there is no word after three months, you could query by mail (with another SASE) or phone, but in my opinion you should give it up and go on to other magazines. Some of them, alas, get a kick out of making serious, well-intentioned people squirm.

What if after a number of submissions it turns out that nobody wants your work, does that mean it's no good? Not at all. Provided that someone of discernment has liked something about your work, it simply means that the milieu you thought you belonged to is inappropriate or is not ready to accept you yet. You must either go back to the Dustbook directory and begin looking for magazines of a different type—or get some friends together and found a magazine of your own! That's how most of them got started—no one wanted the work of the editors and his or her friends. And that's how some of them got to be so snotty—they're doing unto others what has been done to them!

Make no mistake about it, founding and running a magazine, on no matter how modest a scale, is hard work. Added to that, it will require money, and may mean that you will have to acquire a number of new skills. Consequently, may I recommend that you seek out COSMEP (the Committee of Small Magazine Editors and Presses) at Box 703, San Francisco, CA 94101, not only for membership but advice. Another aid is a book on how to do it yourself; I prefer *The Self-Publishing*

Manual by Dan Poynter, which takes you through the process step-by-step, providing model letters and the like. Dan will also answer queries, but don't be a free-loader—buy one of his other books.

One matter that you will have to decide early is whether to design and typeset the magazine yourself or have this done by professionals. Consult with your local copy shop and computer shop and compare their prices: will it be worthwhile to buy your own computer and typesetting program, invest the time learning how they operate and then using them? If you decide that it is, be advised that typesetting programs like Ventura Publisher, QuarkExpress, and Aldus Pagemaker come with style sheets or grids for magazines and newsletters to make the job simpler.

Once you have ten poems accepted or in print, you should apply for membership in the national organization Poets & Writers, which furnishes all kinds of information and services, including a directory in which you will be listed. Their address is 72 Spring Street, New York, NY 10013, telephone (212) 226-3586.

At the same time you should begin trying to find a publisher for a book of your poems, which means going back yet once more to the Dustbook directory and beginning the process of query and submission all over again, this time with a view to ferreting out book publishers who might be interested. Send a good selection of poems, including published and unpublished ones, and be sure to include in your cover letter a list of magazines where your works have appeared.

The same holds true for book publishers as for magazines—if you don't achieve success after a certain number of submissions, consider founding your own small press. And once again, you should make a considered decision as to whether you want to do the production "in house" or farm it out to freelancers. If you decide on the former, Ventura Publisher 4.1.1 is definitely the program for you. However, you are going to have to design your book first: decide on the size of the pages, what is going to appear on them besides poems (headers, for example), and so on. So before getting too far along, you should make thumbnail sketches of pages, including title page, table of contents, and index of first lines, and work up a "dummy" of the whole book. In order to do so with less fuss than you now anticipate, I suggest that you consult Malcolm Barker's *Book Design & Production for the Small Publisher* (San Francisco: Londonborn, 1990), which gives an excellent overview, and Stanley Rice's *Book Design: Text Format Models* (New York: Bowker, 1978), especially Chapter 7, which covers the typesetting of poetry.

When your book of poems comes out, go to your favorite literary bookstore and introduce yourself if you haven't already done so—feel them out to see if they will carry your book. They might even be willing to hold a "pub" party for you, at which you would read from your new book and autograph copies for purchasers. But don't be surprised or hurt if they turn you down—bookstores are hard-pressed these days and they may not want to take on the work of a new writer who has no following. If that turns out to be the case or there is no such establishment near you, have a friend or friends host a party in one of their homes and see Poynter's book about how to sell your book by mail.

No matter who publishes your first book of poems, you are going to have to try to get it reviewed. Reviews, regardless of what they say, are advertisements; even a bad review sells books. So don't worry about sending to people who will be nice. Do be concerned about making the review copy of your book count—that is, having it receive some attention from a newspaper or magazine whose audience is larger than its staff. Yes, you guessed it—it's back to the Dustbook directory and Dan Poynter for you, and there will be more cover letters for you to write, more packages to send out, and more waiting.

Another way of getting the news out about your book of poems is to do readings at local libraries and schools, and here, if you feel gun-shy, the drama teacher at your local community college or high school might come in handy to coach you in your delivery. Poets & Writers provides small matching grants to poets for readings if the organizations for which they perform pay.

Small-press book fairs, both on a local and national level, should not be neglected either. Urge your publisher to rent a table, or if you are self-published, consider sharing one with someone else in the same situation. Be sure that excerpts from your book reviews are on display, perhaps mounted on a board.

Finally, you may want to absent yourself for a spell from the place where you earn your daily bread and simply write, and for this there are foundations that give grants. If you like being among other artists, including some who have really made it, there are art colonies. Query Poets & Writers or see your friendly reference librarian for up-to-date lists.

OTHER DIRECTIONS YOU MIGHT WANT TO TAKE—LIKE WAY OUT

Let's face it, with the advent of TV and computers, each year sees fewer and fewer readers of anything except information or trash. Reading for pleasure seems to be on the way out or in a kind of eclipse. So instead of being a Rip Van Winkle malcontent, why not try to appeal to people with highly developed visual or auditory noodles?

With respect to the visual, one simple way is to turn your poems into designs using the letters. Known as concrete poetry, such forms have been around as far back at least as George Herbert (1593–1633). Look, for instance, at what he did with a poem entitled "Easter Wings":

> Lord, who createdst man in wealth and store,
>   Though foolishly he lost the same,
>   Decaying more and more
>   Till he became
>   Most poor:
>   With thee
>   O let me rise
>   As larks, harmoniously,
>   And sing this day thy victories:
> Then shall the fall further the flight in me.
>
> My tender age in sorrow did begin;
>   And still with sicknesses and shame
>   Thou didst so punish sin,
>   That I became
>   Most thin.
>   With thee
>   Let me combine,
>   And feel this day thy victory;
>   For, if I *imp* my wing on thine,   *graft*
> Affliction shall advance the flight in me.

The best news is that you don't have to own any high-tech equipment to create such a design; a simple typewriter will do the trick. To see what I mean, sit down at the old clunker and spend a few minutes re-creating "Easter Wings."

Some tips for doing this successfully: begin by setting your right and left margins equally. This can be at zero, a half inch, one inch, or what you will as long as there is ample horizontal space for your lines of text. Roll in a sheet of paper and start, let's say, one inch down. Don't worry about the vertical placement of your poem-design, as that can be corrected on the copy machine. Also, don't be gun-shy about making typing mistakes, as there is always opaquing fluid and correction tape (or, as in the good old days, an ink eraser or some clear fluid in a little bottle that smelled suspiciously like laundry bleach). If you feel uneasy and really only want to experiment at first, use the backs of old 8½" x 11" correspondence and such. To keep the typewriter roller free of ink, roll in two sheets back to back.

The first line of your text should be centered. To do this, bring your typewriter carriage clear to the left and tap on the space bar, counting taps, until you reach as far as the carriage will go on the right. Subtract from this number the total number of characters and spaces of the first line of "Easter Wings," or 43, and then divide the result in half. Bring your carriage way to the left again and tap that number of spaces with the space bar, and then begin typing. *Voilà*, your line should be centered; if not, try again.

If you look at the text of "Easter Wings," you'll see that the second line starts three spaces to the right of the first; do likewise, and continue on with the succeeding lines.

When your poem-design is typed the way it should be, you might want to put a border around it. I always experiment by cutting a rectangle the size of the poem out of another piece of scrap paper and slowly enlarging it until I have an opening that suits me. Borders can be drawn with a ruler or typed in with the underline key; interesting effects can be obtained by using a line of asterisks (*****), ampersands (&&&&&&), or other characters. If you want to get really cute, try varying a character (a question mark, for instance) up and down or combining two or more characters (# + + +# + + +# + + + or /.^./.^./.^.); just a few periods to separate a single character can add something (!..!..!..!).

For a final touch, shade in the background of your poem with a colored pencil or some watercolor; "Easter Wings" might look very good against pale blue.

It is also possible to enhance your poems visually by combining each on a page with a photo or a drawing. If you're not an able photographer, you can photocopy a suitable photo from a magazine or book, borrow one from the picture collection of a large public library, or even rent one for one-time use from an agency like The Bettman Archive, 902 Broadway, New York, NY 10036, telephone (212) 777-6200. Whatever your source, do be sure to credit it somewhere on your page.

Finding an appropriate drawing may turn out to be a little easier: there's a whole realm of art, fine and not so fine, that is in the public domain and known as clip-art. Most art supply stores carry a copious supply of clip-art books nowadays; if yours does not, write for a catalog from Dover Publications, Inc.,   31 East Second Street, Mineola, NY 11501, which puts out most of them.

To place your photo or drawing tastefully on a page with your poem, you may want to make some thumbnail sketches first, in which you treat the text and visual material as rectangles. If you can't decide among several arrangements, ask someone to lend a hand; for instance, you might ask the person behind the counter in your local copy shop, who spends whole days aligning type and may have a well-developed eye for that kind of task. Books on layout and design, which tend to be rather technical, may also be of help here.

Of course, if you own or have access to a computer—whether it be a PC or a Mac—with a scanner and a drawing program, the task is infinitely easier and the possibilities of combining your poem with graphics almost endless. Not only can you change the size and shape of your graphic and shift it around on the page, you can also set the text of your poem in an appropriate typeface and scale it up or down.

To give an example, using CorelDRAW!3, one of the best drawing programs around for the PC, I created the following, from Milton's "l'Allegro," for my 1995 novel *Bagatelle • Guinevere*:

```
        *
   *         *      *
Hence  loathed  Melancholy
Of  Cerberus  and  blackest  midnight  born,  *
In  Stygian  caves  forlorn  *
'Mongst  horrid  shapes  and  shrieks,  and  sights  unholy.  *
     *         *      *      *
        *         *      *         *
```

The typeface, supplied by CorelDRAW!, is called Jasper, and I used Star #63 in Star series 1 in their graphics list. After putting the text and stars together, I saved them in an EPS (encapsulated postscript file) for use in a typesetting program. The blessing of this is that when importing it into a typesetting program, you can increase or decrease the height (and therefore the type size).

To belabor this a bit, I began by typing my text and duplicating it a half dozen times. Then I went through the list of typefaces in CorelDRAW!'s list and changed each set of lines into one that struck my fancy and seemed right. When printing out the page, I saw at once that Jasper was the most suitable typeface and tried the text in different sizes of the same from 11 to 16 points before settling on 14.

My next job was to find a star that worked with it, which meant simply looking at each star in turn in the two CorelDRAW! series. The stars' sizes were varied by either choosing a point size in the menu or using the mouse to push and pull on the star's horizontal and vertical handles when I had the star on the screen. Once my stars were the right size, I duplicated them and shifted them around the text until I had a satisfactory arrangement. It may sound more complicated than it actually is—as with most computer projects, what's needed is neither brains nor skill, but patience!

Here is another graphically enhanced poem that I created for my novel *Bagatelle • Guinevere*. It's my rendering of Gilgamesh's return to Uruk, his hometown, after a grueling trip to the underworld in which he left behind his best friend, Enkidu:

> ✸ ✸ ✸ ✸ ✸ ✸ ✸
> Run, ferryman, run. Go run.
> See if my city, my Uruk's still there. Is
>   everything as I left it?
> Of good baked brick were the walls.
>   Clever men contrived them.
> Part of it inside was garden, another
>   part field, and then there was the
>   precinct of Ishtar. ✸ ✸ ✸ ✸ ✸ ✸ ✸

The typeface I used here is called President, and I chose it because it reminded me of cuneiform, the wedge-shaped writing on clay that was native to the ancient Near East. I decided on that particular star—#92 of Series 1—because it suggested the rosette, which was used ubiquitously as an ornament at the time, and I deliberately kept each line of "rosettes" uneven as a further reminder of those days when ornamentation was done by hand and such unevenness was the rule rather than the exception.

Once you have your poems combined with photos or drawings, see if some nearby business establishment, such as a coffeehouse or bank, is willing to display your creations; if you really feel confident about them, try an actual art gallery! I'm going to use mine—there are 20-odd in *Bagatelle • Guinevere*—on postcards and note papers, appropriately surrounded by a border. Of course, when it comes to bordering something on the computer, there is such a wide range of widths, textures, and patterns to choose from that it boggles the mind.

To get a good print of your typeset poem with graphic images, you're going to have to use a postscript printer, which has a very high price tag. I suggest that you check with your local copy shop, which may have one for rent by the hour or know where this printing can be done.

As for appealing to people through the ear, I have already mentioned going out and giving readings. If you do so, you might want to get your audience involved by making some response like clapping in time with you or even repeating things aloud after you. You could also add suitable background music to your reading or even have a poem or poems set to music. This can be done with some piece from the past or with a new one written just for you (by a composer friend you met at one of those art colonies, for instance). But either way it's likely to cost you something, and then you're going to have to chant or sing—and that's going to mean more lessons, unless, of course, you get a singer. If you tape your new creations and they have appeal, some DJ might be willing to play a selection or two over his or her radio station—who knows, a record company might be persuaded to market your work in that form.

The be-all and end-all would be a multimedia show involving a combination of any of the above on videotape with a full airing over your local PBS station.

Good luck!

But of course through all of the aforementioned trials and tribulations one keeps on writing—because one enjoys it.

Contemporary female poets have perhaps had more than their share of say in this chapter, so let it end as the book began, with a few well-chosen words by Harvey Shapiro:

DOMESTIC MATTERS

It wasn't what I had thought—
Children taking up
Most of the house, leaving
Me (or so it often seems)
Only room enough
For the bed. Which itself
Is a kind of relic, as if
From an earlier
Marriage. And so you turn
In the bedroom door,
White, and so small,
To say good night.
To say there are
Two of us.

I am crying over this body of yours
Which is to wither in the dust.
Already your belly's thrust outpoints
Your breasts. The hair of your head
Grows thin. A skeleton
Smiles to me with your gums.

We are almost
Out of earshot
Of one another
Yet our answers
Seem to find
Connected questions
Of an urgency
So deep, they might
Be coming
From the center
Of a life.

We were comrades
In a disastrous war.
We have created a history
That will be sung
In the psyche of others.
Troy's burning
And the flames may light us
All the way to death.

SUBMITTING YOUR WORK

The following is a list of general literary magazines and journals that do not have any requirements as to a poem's style or subject matter and seem to have a real welcoming hand extended to new and emerging poets. For periodicals with more specialized interests (e.g., environmental, erotic, ethnic, feminist, gay, regional, etc.), see the subject headings in the Dust and CLMP directories.

Incidentally, if anybody on the staff of the magazines listed below treats you or your work disrespectfully without cause, I would like to hear about it.

Agni
Askold Melnyczuk, Editor
Boston University Creative Writing Program
236 Bay State Road
Boston, MA 02215
Established: 1972
Circulation: 1500
Publishes: twice a year
Format: 5½" x 8½", 250–320 pages
Submit: Oct 1 to May 1

The Beloit Poetry Journal
Marion K. Stocking, Editor
Box 154, RFD2
Ellsworth, ME 04605
Established: 1950
Circulation: 1500
Publishes: four times a year
Format: 5½" x 8½", 48 pages
Submit: Any time

The Berkeley Poetry Review
Connie Vallejo, Editor
700 Eshleman Hall
University of California
Berkeley, CA 94720
Established: 1973
Circulation: 500 to 1000
Publishes: once or twice a year
Format: 5½" x 8½", 120–150 pages
Submit: Any time

Black River Review
Deborah G. Gilbert, Editor
855 Mildred Avenue
Lorain, OH 44052
Established: 1985
Circulation: 400
Publishes: once a year
Format: 8½" x 11", 60 pages
Submit: Between January 1 and May 1 only

Blue Unicorn
Ruth G. Iodice, Editor
22 Avon Road
Kensington, CA 94707
Established: 1977
Circulation: 500
Publishes: three times a year
Format: 4¼" x 5½", 56–60 pages
Submit: Any time

Cafe Solo
Glenna Luschei, Editor
c/o City Books
1111 East Carson Street
Pittsburgh, PA 15203
Established: 1969
Circulation: 500
Publishes: three times a year
Format: 8½" x 11", 44 pages
Submit: Any time

The Cathartic
Patrick M. Ellingham, Editor
POB 1391
Fort Lauderdale, FL 33302
Established: 1974
Publishes: twice a year
Circulation: 200–300
Format: 5½" x 8½", 28 pages
Submit: Any time

The Chattahoochee Review
Lamar York, Editor
DeKalb College
2101 Womack Road
Dunwoody, GA 30338-4497
Established: 1980
Publishes: four times a year
Circulation: 1250
Format: 6" x 9", 100 pages
Submit: Any time

CPQ
John M. Brander, Editor
1200 E. Ocean Blvd., #64
Long Beach, CA 90802
Established: 1972
Publishes: three or four times a year
Circulation: 500
Format: 6" x 9", 84 pages
Submit: Any time

Crazyhorse
Ralph Burns, Poetry Editor
English Department
University of Arkansas at Little Rock
2801 S. University
Little Rock, AR 72204
Established: 1960
Publishes: twice a year
Circulation: 1000
Format: 6" x 9", 135 pages
Submit: Any time

The Cream City Review
Sandra Nelson, Editor-in-Chief
POB 413
University of Wisconsin-Milwaukee
Milwaukee, WI 53201
Established: 1975
Publishes: twice a year
Circulation: 2000
Format: 5½" x 8½", 300 pages
Submit: Any time

Embers
Katrina Van Tassel, Editor
Box 404
Guilford, CT 06437
Established: 1979
Publishes: twice a year
Circulation: 500
Format: 6" x 9", 48 pages
Submit: Any time

Folio
Department of Literature
American University
Washington, DC 20016
Established: 1984
Publishes: twice a year
Circulation: 400
Format: 6" x 9", 70 pages
Submit: August to April

For Poets Only
L.M. Walsh, Editor
POB 4855
Schenectady, NY 12304
Established: 1985
Publishes: four times a year
Circulation: 150
Format: 5½" x 8", 30 pages
Submit: Any time

Green Mountains Review
Neil Shepard
Johnson State College
Johnson, VT 05656
Established: 1987
Publishes: twice a year
Circulation: 1000
Format: 6" x 9", 120+ pages
Submit: Any time

Hanging Loose
Robert Hershon
231 Wyckoff Street
Brooklyn, NY 11217
Established: 1966
Publishes: three times a year
Circulation: 1500
Format: 7" x 8½", 96 pages
Submit: Any time

Long Pond Review
Russell Steinke
Suffolk Community College
533 College Road
Selden, NY 11784
Established: 1975
Publishes: once a year
Circulation: 500
Format: 6" x 9", 72–88 pages
Submit: Any time

Manhattan Poetry Review
Elaine Reiman-Fenton
FDR Box 8207
New York, NY 10150
Established: 1982
Publishes: twice a year
Circulation: 500–1000
Format: 5½" x 8½", 52–60 pages
Submit: Any time

New Delta Review
Randi Gray
Department of English
Louisiana State University
Baton Rouge, LA 70803-5001
Established: 1984
Publishes: twice a year
Circulation: 500
Format: 6" x 9", 112 pages
Submit: Any time

New Laurel Review
Lee Meitzen Grue
828 Lesseps Street
New Orleans, LA 70117
Established: 1971
Publishes: once a year
Circulation: 500
Format: 6" x 9", 85 pages
Submit: September through May

New Myths: MSS
Robert Mooney
SUNY-Binghampton
Box 530
Binghampton, NY 13901
Established: 1961
Publishes: twice a year
Circulation: 1000
Format: 6" x 9", 200 pages
Submit: Any time

Piedmont Literary Review
Gail White
Piedmont Literary Society
1017 Spanish Moss Lane
Breaux Bridge, LA 70517
Established: 1976
Publishes: four times a year
Circulation: 300
Format: 5½" x 8½", 50 pages
Submit: Any time

Pivot
Martin Mitchell
250 Riverside Drive, #23
New York, NY 10025
Established: 1951
Publishes: once a year
Circulation: 1500–3000
Format: 6" x 9", 76 pages
Submit: January 1 to June 1

Prairie Schooner
Hilda Raez
201 Andrews Hall
University of Nebraska
Lincoln, NE 68588-0334
Established: 1927
Publishes: four times a year
Circulation: 3100
Format: 6" x 9", 176 pages
Submit: Any time

Rambunctious Review
M. Dellutri
1221 West Pratt Boulevard
Chicago, IL 60626
Established: 1986
Publishes: once a year
Circulation: 450
Format: 7 x 10, 48 pages
Submit: Any time

Shenandoah
Dabney Stuart
POB 722
Lexington, VA 24450
Established: 1950
Publishes: four times a year
Circulation: 2100
Format: 6" x 9", 120 pages
Submit: Any time

The Small Pond Magazine, Inc.
Napoleon St. Cyr
POB 664
Stratford, CT 06497
Established: 1964
Publishes: three times a year
Circulation: 300
Format: 5½" x 8½", 40 pages
Submit: Any time

Sou'wester
Fred W. Robbins
School of Humanities
Southern Illinois University
Edwardsville, IL 62026-1438
Established: 1960
Publishes: three times a year
Circulation: 300
Format: 6" x 9", 84 pages
Submit: Any time

Sycamore Review
Linda Haynes
Department of English
Purdue University
West Lafayette, IN 47907
Established: 1989
Publishes: twice a year
Circulation: 600–700
Format: 6" x 9", 128 pages
Submit: Any time

Turnstile
George White
175 Fifth Avenue, Suite 2348
New York, NY 10010
Established: 1988
Publishes: twice a year
Circulation: 1200
Format: 6" x 9", 128 pages
Submit: Any time

Whole Notes
Nancy Peters Hastings
POB 1374
Las Cruces, NM 88004
Established: 1984
Publishes: twice a year
Circulation: 400
Format: 5½" x 8½", 18 pages
Submit: Any time

The William and Mary Review
Stacy Payne
POB 8795
The College of William and Mary
Williamsburg, VA 23187-8795
Established: 1962
Publishes: once a year
Circulation: 3500
Format: 6" x 9", 120 pages
Submit: Any time

BIBLIOGRAPHY

ANTHOLOGIES

1. GENERAL

Allison, Alexander, et al., eds. *The Norton Anthology of Poetry*. 4th ed. New York: Norton, 1989.

Bate, Walter Jackson, and David Perkins, eds. *British and American Poets: Chaucer to the Present*. New York: Harcourt, 1986.

Gardner, Helen, ed. *The New Oxford Book of English Verse*. New York: Oxford University Press, 1978.

Nims, Frederick, ed. *The Harper Anthology of Poetry*. New York: Harper & Row, 1981.

Rosenthal, M.L. *Poetry in English: An Anthology*. New York: Oxford University Press, 1987.

2. MODERN

Elmann, Richard, ed. *The Norton Anthology of Modern Poetry*. New York: Norton, 1973.

Poulin, Al., Jr., ed. *Contemporary American Poetry*. Boston: Houghton Mifflin, 1985.

3. THE CONTEMPORARY POETS FEATURED IN THIS BOOK

Fainlight, Ruth. *A Forecast, a Fable*. London: Outpost Publications, 1958.

————— , —————. *Cages*. Chester Springs, PA: Dufour, 1966 and London: Macmillan, 1966.

————— , —————. *Eighteen Poems from 1966*. London: Turret Books, 1967.

————— , —————. *To See the Matter Clearly*. London: Macmillan, 1968 and Chester Springs, PA: Dufour, 1969.

————— , —————. *Poems* (with Ted Hughes and Alan Sillitoe). London: Rainbow Press, 1971.

————— , —————. *The Region's Violence*. London: Hutchinson, 1973.

————— , —————. *Twenty-one Poems*. London: Turret Books, 1973.

————— , —————. *Another Full Moon*. London: Hutchinson, 1976.

————— , —————. *Sibyls and Others*. London: Hutchinson, 1980.

————— , —————. *Climates*. London: Bloodaxe Books, 1983.

————— , —————. *Fifteen to Infinity*. London: Hutchinson, 1983 and Pittsburgh: Carnegie-Mellon University Press, 1986.

————— , —————. *Selected Poems*. London: Hutchinson, 1988.

————— , —————. *The Knot*. London: Hutchinson, 1990.

————— , —————. *Sybils*. Searsmont, ME: Gehenna Press, 1991.

————— , —————. *This Time of Year*. London: Sinclair-Stenson, 1994.

Inez, Colette. *The Woman Who Loved Worms*. New York: Doubleday, 1972.
————— , —————. *Alive and Taking Names*. Columbus, OH: Ohio University Press, 1977.
————— , —————. *Getting Under Way: New and Selected Poems*. Brownsville, Ore: Story Line Press, 1993.
————— , —————. *For Reasons of Music*. Memphis, TN: Ion Books, 1994.
————— , —————. *Naming the Moons*. Lewisburg, PA: Apple Alley Press, 1994.
————— , —————. *Eight Minutes from the Sun*. Upper Montclair, NJ: Saturday Press, 1983.
————— , —————. *Family Life*. Santa Cruz, CA: Story Line Press, 1988.
Miller, Walter James. *Making an Angel*. New York: Pylon Press, 1977.
Shapiro, Harvey. *The Eye*. Denver, CO: Swallow Press, 1953.
————— , —————. *Mountain, Fire, Thornbush*. Denver, CO: Swallow Press, 1961.
————— , —————. *Battle Report*. Middletown, CT: Wesleyan University Press, 1966.
————— , —————. *This World*. Middletown, CT: Wesleyan University Press, 1971.
————— , —————. *Lauds & Nightsounds*. New York: SUN, 1978.
————— , —————. *The Light Holds*. Middletown, CT: Wesleyan University Press, 1984.
————— , —————. *National Cold Storage Company: New and Selected Poems*. Middletown, CT. Wesleyan UP, 1988.
————— , —————. *A Day's Portion*. Brooklyn, NY: Hanging Loose Press, 1994.

Books About How to Write Poetry

Dessner, Lawrence J. *How to Write a Poem*. New York: NYU Press, 1979.
Drake, Barbara. *Writing Poetry*. New York: Harcourt, 1983.
Lewis, Patricia. *A Guide to Writing Prize-Winning Poems*. Carlstadt, NJ: Rainbow, 1984.
Riccio, Ottone M. *The Intimate Art of Writing Poems*. Englewood Cliffs, NJ: Prentice Hall, 1980.
Roberston, Pauline. *Poetry Writing Self-Taught*. Amarillo, TX: Paramount TX, 1988.
Turco, Lewis. *Poetry: An Introduction Through Writing*. New York: Reston, 1973.

Rhyming Dictionaries

Espy, Willard R. *Words to Rhyme With*. New York: Facts on File, 1986.
Fergusson, Rosalind. *The Penguin Rhyming Dictionary*. New York: Viking, 1985.
Johnson, Burges. *New Rhyming Dictionary and Poet's Handbook*. New York: Harper, 1957.

Stillman, Francis, and Whitefield, Jane. *Poet's Manual and Rhyming Dictionary*. New York: Crowell, 1965.

Wood, Clement. *Complete Rhyming Dictionary*. New York: Doubleday, 1936.

MANUSCRIPT PREPARATION

A Manual of Style. Chicago: University of Chicago Press, 1961.

Achtert, Walter S., and Joseph Gibaldi. *The MLA Style Manual*. New York: MLA, 1985.

Osley, Carol A. *How to Properly Prepare Poems*. Mohawk, NY: Soco, 1983.

PUBLISHING

Barker, Malcolm. *Book Design & Production for the Small Publisher*. San Francisco: Londonborn, 1990.

Directory of Poetry Publishers. Paradise, CA: Dustbooks, 1989.

Poet's Market. Cincinnati: Writer's Digest, 1985.

Poynter, Dan. *The Self-Publishing Manual: How to Write, Print, and Sell Your Own Book*. Santa Barbara: Para, 1989.

Rice, Stanley. *Book Design: Text Format Models*. New York: Bowker, 1978.

BOOKS ABOUT PROSODY OR THE MECHANICS OF POETRY

Deutsch, Babette. *Poetry Handbook*. New York: Harper & Row, 1974.

Fussell, Paul, Jr. *Poetic Meter and Poetic Form*. New York: Random House, 1965.

Jerome, Judson. *The Poet's Handbook*. New York: Writer's Digest Books, 1980.

Malof, Joseph. *A Manual of English Meters*. Bloomington: Indiana University Press, 1970.

Packard, William. *The Poet's Dictionary: A Handbook of Prosody and Poetic Devices*. New York: Harper & Row, 1989.

Preminger, Alex, ed. *Princeton Encyclopedia of Poetry and Poetics*. Princeton: Princeton UP, 1974.

Saintsbury, George. *A History of English Prosody from the Twelfth Century to the Present*. New York: Russell, 1961.

Shapiro, Karl, and Breun, Robert. *A Prosody Handbook*. New York: Harper & Row, 1965.

Turco, Lewis. *The Book of Forms: A Handbook of Poetics*. New York: Dutton, 1968.

Williams, Miller. *Patterns of Poetry: An Encyclopedia of Forms*. Baton Rouge: U. of LA Press, 1986.

Wood, Clement. *The Poet's Handbook*. New York: World, 1940.

OTHER WORKS CITED

Bogen, Nancy. *Bagatelle • Guinevere*. New York: Twickenham, 1995.

Bogen, Nancy. *Klytaimnestra Who Stayed at Home*. New York: Lintel, 1989.

Corbett, Fdward P. *Classical Rhetoric for the Modern Student*. New York: Oxford University Press, 1965.

Edman, Irwin. *Arts and the Man*. New York: Mentor, 1949.

Frye, Northrop. *Anatomy of Criticism*. Princeton: Princeton University Press, 1957.

Holman, C. Hugh, and William Harmon. *A Handbook to Literature*. New York: Macmillan, 1986.

Melville, Herman. *Moby-Dick*. New York: Norton, 1967.

Percy, Thomas. *Reliques of Ancient English Poetry*. London: Bell, 1900.

Santayana, George. *The Sense of Beauty*. New York: Modern Library, 1955.

"HOW TO" GUIDES

AVAILABLE AT BOOKSTORES EVERYWHERE

MACMILLAN • USA